# Already Sanctified

# Already Sanctified

## A Theology of the Christian Life in Light of God's Completed Work

Don J. Payne

BakerAcademic
a division of Baker Publishing Group
Grand Rapids, Michigan

Published by Baker Academic
a division of Baker Publishing Group
PO Box 6287, Grand Rapids, MI 49516-6287
www.bakeracademic.com

Printed and bound by CPI Group (UK) Ltd, Croydon, CR0 4YY



Library of Congress Cataloging-in-Publication Data
Names: Payne, Don J. (Donny Joe), author.
Title: Already sanctified : a theology of the Christian life in light of God's completed work / Don J. Payne.
Description: Grand Rapids, MI : Baker Academic, a division of Baker Publishing Group, 2020. | Includes bibliographical references and index.
Identifiers: LCCN 2019040902 | ISBN 9781540961303 (paperback)
Subjects: LCSH: Sanctification.
Classification: LCC BT765 .P39 2020 | DDC 234/.8—dc23
LC record available at https://lccn.loc.gov/2019040902

ISBN: 978-1-5409-6313-0 (casebound)



20 21 22 23 24 25 26 7 6 5 4 3 2 1

To Thomas A. Noble,
whose life and scholarship
embody the artful synthesis
of grace and rigor that reflects
God's sanctifying presence.

# Contents

# Acknowledgments

The list of people who have influenced this project could almost be a chapter in itself. Even to attempt giving proper credit is to risk the embarrassment of overlooking someone. To those whose names I forgot to mention, I beg their forgiveness and hope they will know of my gratitude.

The unnamed include a long train of students, colleagues, and friends who have sharpened my thinking on the subject of sanctification with their patient listening, insightful questions, affirmation, quizzical expressions, and disagreement. I am grateful to the board and administration of Denver Seminary for a generous sabbatical to focus on this work. Two deans under whom it has been my privilege to serve, Dr. Randy MacFarland and Dr. Lynn Cohick, have been particularly encouraging.

For twenty-one years Denver Seminary has proven to be a most congenial and fertile environment for theological work such as this. Across the institution—board, administration, faculty, and staff—numerous individuals have offered more than merely polite interest and encouragement for this project. I honestly cannot think of a place I would rather serve or better colleagues with whom to serve.

A special thanks to four who devoted significant measures of their personal time to reading and commenting on an early and extremely rough draft of the manuscript: Laura Flanders, Andrew Hay, Knut Heim, and Jim Howard. I make no claims for the finished product, but it is better by far than it would have been without their insightful input. As much as I would love to divert the blame to them for any shortcomings in the work, alas, I must take responsibility for what I have chosen to say and how I have said it.

Dave and Kathleen Sherman generously, and twice, offered the use of their cabin so that I could write undisturbed. Thanks to Baker Academic and Bob Hosack for accepting this project and to Julie Zahm and others on the editorial team for being so easy to work with throughout the process. My wife, Sharon, deserves my unqualified gratitude (and she actually read the manuscript). She has relentlessly believed in me and encouraged me. More than any person I know, she embodies what I argue for in this book. Theologians should always look for experiential validation of their claims, and she is my source of that in this case.

Finally, thanks to our sanctifying God, whose gracious, empowering presence I have sought and relied on, in hopes that this book will shine a glimmer of encouraging light on what it means to have been made holy.

# Introduction

For those who try to be serious about the Christian faith, the subject of sanctification can be inspiring, intimidating, intriguing, puzzling, frustrating, or guilt-inducing—or all of these on different days! Why another book on sanctification when so much has already been written about this doctrine?

For centuries the doctrine of sanctification has been a theological battleground. Interest in sanctification stretches across disciplinary lines, perhaps because it seems to have more immediate and practical bearing on every Christian's life, including the personal lives of the scholars who write about it. For at least that reason the doctrine of sanctification holds widespread interest for Christians of all traditions and in all places.

With or without the technical, scholarly vocabulary, our beliefs about sanctification affect how we live in response to God and others. They directly relate to the first and greatest commandment and the second commandment, as Jesus stated them: "You shall love the Lord your God with all your heart, and with all your soul, and with all your mind" and "You shall love your neighbor as yourself" (Matt. 22:37, 39). Those who take these words seriously face the lifelong task of working out the possibilities and practicalities of those words in both the interior and the exterior domains of life.

Since the language of sanctification or holiness often depicts the nature and pursuit of these goals, questions and challenges continue to arise. What is a holy person and how do I (and we) become holy? What is my role and what is God's role? What do my failures, shortcomings, and ongoing struggles mean for my relationship with God? Where do I find the resources for faithfulness to God even through failure, discouragement, and seeming lack of progress? What should be my expectations for spiritual growth and transformation, especially in light of chronic struggles and areas of bondage? Christians routinely ask at least some of these questions in one form or another. These constitute, or at least illustrate, some of the challenges of sanctification—what it means to be holy.

Ambiguities, tensions, and challenges will never go away entirely until the Lord returns. However, some symptoms that commonly encumber the faith journey stem from inherited patterns of reading the biblical texts about sanctification. Those patterns include underattending to some aspects of sanctification while overdeveloping others. This has resulted in a sort of chronic disproportioning of the doctrine that, like some physical abnormalities, can seriously affect one's stride. Every bit as serious, this disproportioning has become so familiar that it seems not to be recognized as problematic.

The complex challenges involved in the doctrine of sanctification require patient reexamination of the biblical material, honest identification of assumptions that have been read into certain texts, and particular attention to the pattern of the doctrine as it unfolds and functions in Scripture. What we can find, I contend, is a doctrine of sanctification that is actually encouraging and empowering without being simplistic or formulaic.

Questions and controversies about what it means to be sanctified tend to fall into some general categories. Is it already completed and behind us? If so, how do we not become morally complacent? Is it primarily something out in front of us and out of reach within this lifetime? If so, how is it meaningfully to be pursued and can assurance ever realistically come our way? What role do other grand biblical themes such as grace and faith play in sanctification?

The dizzying array of opinions on the subject is matched only by the complexities and enigmas within our personal experiences. At the practical level, all Christians have a theology of sanctification that undergirds the ways we actually try to live out our faith, or think we ought to do so. Our practical theologies of sanctification powerfully influence our lives, whatever language we use for it.

This book addresses the need for a constantly renewed theology of the Christian life. Like many significant subjects, this is as complex as the people involved. Thus, the definitive and "last word" on sanctification may never be written. That's all the more reason to write another one: to keep probing and inching our way incrementally toward whatever clarity God will grant us on a subject that affects the core of our relationships with both God and others.

I know the need for this clarity first and foremost as a Christian for whom the subject of the Christian life has been central—always challenging and often problematic—as long as I have been a consciously committed Christian (at least forty-six years at the time of this writing). That's a reasonably lengthy stretch of time in which to ponder what it means to live the Christian life—to be holy. Eight years of pastoral ministry and over twenty years on a seminary faculty have confirmed my experience as typical. For countless people the Christian life is alternatingly glorious and grinding, though the descriptions of that experience vary among different Christian traditions. However we express those experiences, everyone who claims to be a Christian—a follower of Jesus Christ—thinks about, or should think about, what it means to be holy.

In the introduction to their book on sanctification, my friends Kent Eilers and Kyle Strobel offer the following keen observation: "'The Christian life' is theological shorthand for redeemed human existence in communion with the triune God through union with Christ in the Spirit. . . . To state it another way, to address 'the Christian life' is to speak about the character of reconciled and renewed human existence."[1] That description covers a lot of theological ground, gives me hope, and helps frame what I want to explore in this book. The concept of sanctification may always mystify and challenge us, but it can also be life-giving and compelling. Especially if discussions of holiness have not generally been life-giving and compelling for you the reader, then I encourage you to keep reading.

1. Eilers and Strobel, *Sanctified by Grace*, 3.

## Preliminaries

We must reexamine how sanctification actually functions in the Christian life, particularly with respect to growth and transformation. The scope of this reexamination is limited to a specific, often overlooked and underdeveloped aspect of sanctification: that which Scripture presents as already having taken place. Some call it "positional." I prefer the descriptor "accomplished," though with the important qualification that the term does not imply any particular experience, any sort of perfection in personal character, or an achieved level of spiritual maturity. I contend that the accomplished aspect of sanctification holds far more power than has often been acknowledged and defines how other aspects of sanctification should be understood.

Two consequences unfold from having overlooked and underdeveloped the accomplished aspect of the biblical sanctification portrait. One consequence is confusion about what "making holiness perfect" (2 Cor. 7:1) and "be holy" (1 Pet. 1:15–16) mean. Texts such as these are commonly assumed to depict the process of growth in godly character and maturity, often referred to as "progressive sanctification." That assumption dominates many discussions of sanctification and frequently creates a crippling sense of spiritual inadequacy, fatigue, and fear.[2] This is especially the case in light of Hebrews 12:14, which speaks of "holiness without which no one will see the Lord."

A second consequence is inadequate grounding and resourcing for spiritual growth and transformation. I will argue that biblical imperatives for growth and transformation easily become moralistic and disheartening when not properly anchored in God's accomplished, definitive sanctifying work and his upholding of that sanctification by grace through the Holy Spirit.[3]

Few debate that the New Testament portrays the Christian life as a life of growth into maturity, defined by transformation and conformity to the image of Jesus Christ. Growth involves change from

2. Some will contend that these negative effects stem from a misunderstanding of progressive sanctification or other factors that have contributed to such distortions. Yet the possibility of misunderstanding and distortion does not constitute either an adequate exegetical defense or grounds for dismissing such debilitating experiences.

3. Eilers and Strobel, *Sanctified by Grace*, 7–8.

what we are into what we not yet are but were created to be. Though I am not the first to do so, I question the notion that "progressive sanctification" best accounts for the combination of imperatives and yet-to-be-completed sanctification texts in the New Testament. Furthermore, I question whether sanctification is synonymous with the transformation and growth to which believers are clearly called. I contend that sanctification primarily takes place theologically "upstream," with profound implications for Christian growth.

Misappropriation and underappropriation of the accomplished aspect of sanctification tragically cripple and in some cases even distort the process of growth and transformation. Our theology of growth and transformation, both conceptually and practically, will be only as good as our theology of accomplished sanctification. Thus, the church needs an ever-renewed theology of sanctification to resource the personal and pastoral impact that this doctrine has on the lives of all Christians. This doctrinal renewal includes "scrubbing" the terminology of distortions and generalizations that have accumulated over time and created confusion.

A clarified and robust theology of accomplished sanctification can reshape, renew, and resource efforts at "discipleship," the language that has long been used for the process of Christian growth.[4] Accomplished sanctification has just as many implications for "spiritual formation," the language of choice for an increasing number of evangelicals who hunger for more depth, nuance, and texture to their faith development than what "discipleship" seems to provide.[5] A healthy theology of accomplished sanctification can cut through many of the tangles regarding how growth should be pursued and experienced: whether growth is indeed a process or is something more instantaneous, and how conscious effort is involved in growth. This is not an attempt to correct or negate all other perspectives on sanctification, to resolve all the ambiguities and tensions within the

4. See, for example, Hull, *Complete Book of Discipleship*; Harrington and Patrick, *Disciple Maker's Handbook*.

5. See, for example, Demarest, *Satisfy Your Soul*; Demarest, *Seasons of the Soul*. See also Mulholland, *Deeper Journey*. Dallas Willard has provided influential leadership in merging the themes of discipleship and spiritual formation in *Renovation of the Heart* and *The Great Omission*.

doctrine, or eliminate the challenges of living a sanctified life. My central purpose is to provide some perspective on these questions because, despite previous efforts, we are still left with doctrines of sanctification—a "sanctification situation"—that both puzzles and burdens countless believers.[6]

This reexamination of sanctification will first place the doctrine in historical context. Though the doctrine did not originate with the Protestant Reformation, its importance was elevated by that movement. The earliest and most influential Protestant Reformers understood the doctrine of sanctification in somewhat different ways. Yet, each reacted to the particular manner in which late-medieval Roman Catholicism had fused justification and sanctification so as practically to make a person's standing before God contingent on moral performance and progress.

Reformation leaders offered various reconfigurations of the relationship between justification and sanctification. Yet, each insisted on some type of distinction that would preserve the vital biblical notions of salvation *sola gratia* (grace alone) and *sola fidei* (faith alone). Thus, the theological conundrum in the doctrine of sanctification has long revolved, in some fashion, around the question of monergism versus synergism. While justification has been more consistently understood as a monergistic act of God that places a person in a new relationship with God,[7] sanctification has been a far more embattled doctrine among children of the Reformation.[8]

Those historical theological developments significantly influenced readings of the biblical material regarding sanctification and will

6. I have pastored, taught, and counseled these Christians for decades, sharing their befuddlement and discouragement even when I thought I had better answers than I really did.

7. This is the case regardless of where one leans with respect to recent debates over the nature of justification, represented most publicly by N. T. Wright and John Piper. For Wright's view, see *Justification*; for Piper's perspective, see *The Future of Justification*.

8. A pacesetting example of this disagreement occurred in the 1950s when J. I. Packer took issue with the understanding of sanctification popularized by the Keswick movement. See Packer, "'Keswick' and the Reformed Doctrine of Sanctification." Packer argues that sanctification is synergistic contra the monergistic interpretation put forward in Barabas, *So Great Salvation*.

serve as the backdrop for reexamining key texts. The biblical prominence of sanctification is evident from the word groups used for it in Scripture and the frequency with which they occur. Its complexity is demonstrated not so much in ambiguity about the meaning of the words as in the variety of senses in which they are used, how they relate to one another, how they relate to other biblical concepts such as justification and transformation, and how sanctification relates to the varieties of personal experience. Entire sanctification traditions have been defined in part by how they address these matters.

Sanctification can be seen in three general respects, similar to the way Paul presents salvation overall: past or accomplished (e.g., Eph. 2:5, 8: "have been saved"); present (e.g., 1 Cor. 1:18; 2 Cor. 2:15: "are being saved"); and future (e.g., Rom. 5:9: "will be saved"). In this book I argue that accomplished sanctification serves as the dominant and defining sanctification motif in the biblical profile, not to the exclusion or neglect of the other aspects, but that the present and future aspects can be properly understood only in light of what has already been accomplished.

The accomplished nature of sanctification is neither a formal standing nor an acquired level of godly maturity, but rather a definitive and empowering reality that the Holy Spirit has already created in the lives of believers. Quantitatively, the overwhelming majority of New Testament texts related to sanctification refer to it in this manner. Qualitatively, these texts function in a far more straightforward and integrative manner than do the texts that either contain imperatives related to holiness or speak of sanctification as something yet to be realized. Among theological treatments of sanctification that have influenced the broad spectrum of evangelicalism, accomplished ("positional") sanctification has received marginal attention compared to sanctification as something to be pursued and yet to be realized, whether that realization is considered progressive or instantaneous.[9]

9. See, for example, Lewis and Demarest, *Integrative Theology*, 3:195. Lewis and Demarest devote twenty-five pages overall to the biblical doctrine of sanctification. Of these twenty-five pages, one long paragraph connects positional sanctification with regeneration and Spirit-baptism. In a second reference to positional sanctification they relegate it by saying, "Although the [New Testament] literature teaches positional sanctification (Heb. 10:10, 29), it focuses more on the process of growth

Thankfully, the doctrine of sanctification has recently enjoyed renewed attention,[10] much of which has expanded and strengthened its exegetical and theological platform. Little that I offer will be novel or groundbreaking to those whose scholarship precedes and exceeds my own. I simply hope to clarify and work out implications of this key—accomplished—feature in the doctrine of sanctification. The consequences are profound. Just as physical malnutrition can cause various developmental delays, underdevelopment of accomplished sanctification can constrict engagement with the spiritual nutrients necessary for healthy growth in Christlike maturity. This spiritual anemia occurs because the accomplished nature of sanctification represents far more than a positional reality. It is a dynamic act in which God creates everything related to holiness and makes possible everything related to transformation.

## Overview

The approach consists of three major parts. Part 1 surveys the contemporary "sanctification situation" to place this study in historical

toward Christlikeness (2 Peter 3:18; cf. Heb. 10:14; 1 Peter 2:2)" (3:203). Notice that of the three texts cited in support of sanctification as the "process of growth," only Heb. 10:14 employs the ἅγιος word group. F. F. Bruce observes that the present passive participle used there should be understood to depict the believer's "being brought into the perfect relation to God which is involved in the new covenant" (*Epistle to the Hebrews*, 241). Wayne Grudem claims that this beginning stage of sanctification is "roughly equivalent to 'justified' in Paul's vocabulary." Interestingly, Grudem acknowledges much of what I will argue below when he states, "In Hebrews [9:13; 10:10; 13:12] the term *sanctify* . . . is related more to the Old Testament background of ceremonial purity or holiness as necessary for access to God's presence" (*Systematic Theology*, 748n3 [emphasis original]). Yet, he considers this access to God as the "beginning of the Christian life" with the "process that continues throughout our Christian lives" as the "primary sense in which sanctification is used in systematic theology and in Christian conversation generally today" (748). Grudem's treatment of sanctification, while clear about the different senses in which the terminology is used, reflects the common and weakly substantiated assumptions that I wish to challenge regarding which sense dominates, the basis for that dominance, and the implications of that dominance.

10. For examples, see Allen, *Sanctification*; Eilers and Strobel, *Sanctified by Grace*; Kapic, *Sanctification*; Noble, *Holy Trinity: Holy People*; G. Smith, *Called to Be Saints*; Van De Walle, *Rethinking Holiness*; Webster, *Holiness*.

and theological context. The first chapter examines the initial moves made by Martin Luther and John Calvin to clarify the doctrine of sanctification. The second chapter covers some key, post-Reformation, Protestant developments in the doctrine of sanctification and the residual effects of these developments.

Part 2 examines key biblical texts related to the Old Testament practice of consecration (chapter 3) and the New Testament presentation of sanctification. The examination of the New Testament evidence involves particular attention to the *accomplished*, *imperatival*, and *futuristic* aspects of sanctification, looking closely for what these texts do and do not say,[11] and how they function together with the accomplished aspect as the dominant, controlling one. Part 2 also takes into consideration some often overlooked texts and how they contribute to an integrated biblical profile of sanctification. The subject of transformation is considered in light of sanctification as well. A central argument throughout this section is that sanctification and transformation are linked but are not identical; transformation depends on sanctification but should not be confused with it.

Part 3 explores the theological character of sanctification—particularly with the accomplished aspect of sanctification as dominant—and what that implies for personal growth and transformation. This includes connecting accomplished sanctification with other biblical motifs (e.g., union with Christ) to show its animating force.[12]

11. This step will take into account Michael Allen's observation and warning: "Too often, exegetical reasoning can be limited to offering literary and/or theological reflection upon those instances of Holy Scripture that speak directly to a particular theme or topic. Far too frequently, then, a doctrine of sanctification can be bound by those passages and portions of the Bible that employ the idioms of holiness and sanctification alone" (*Sanctification*, 28). With grateful acknowledgment, I will build on David Peterson's exegetical work in *Possessed by God* to develop further some key points and their implications. Though Michael Allen's previously noted observation is in reference to Peterson's work, Peterson is not quite as exegetically myopic as Allen suggests. Peterson admits, "When Paul talks about dying together with Christ and being raised together with him (Rom. 6:1–11), *he expresses the notion of sanctification we have seen elsewhere in his writings*, without specifically using the terminology" (*Possessed by God*, 113 [emphasis original]).

12. Eilers and Strobel reinforce this point and organize the essays in their edited volume accordingly. They note, "The doctrine of the Christian life is informed and illumined by a whole series of theological claims about God, such as his relation

I wish that revisiting and recalibrating the doctrine of sanctification were all it would take to whisk away the relentless challenges of the Christian life: the missteps and dead ends, the setbacks, the dashed expectations, the dark and disorienting days. Yet, that would ignore the wild relational dynamics of this journey that also allow us such joys and delights as come our way. An ever-clarified doctrine of sanctification does not reduce sanctification and transformation to simplistic formulas.

A clarified doctrine of sanctification—defined, sustained, and propelled by accomplished sanctification—does not eliminate struggle, provide shortcuts in the process of spiritual maturation, or induce a supercharged spiritual experience. It does, however, help us better trust the power of what God has already done in and through being present with us in particular ways (not "mere" omnipresence), especially on those occasions when the costs of faithful obedience seem larger than the rewards. It points out the resources and practices that actually contribute to spiritual growth when we are tantalized and then disillusioned by a glitzy menu of seemingly easier tactics.

to created reality, his reconciling works and the human activities which arise from them" (*Sanctified by Grace*, 3).

PART ONE

# How We Got Where We Are

# 1

# The Sanctification Mutiny

What happened with the doctrine of sanctification to get us where we are today? Without rehearsing the full and complex history of the doctrine, we need to understand some key, trajectory-setting moves that shaped the contemporary conversation—and the struggles. Part of that work will be to understand how the "sanctification situation," as we currently experience it, came to be. "Context is everything," as the saying goes.

Proper understanding and assessment of a complex phenomenon demand some knowledge of the backstory, specifically, the factors that contributed to the phenomenon. This holds true for our attempts to make sense of theologies that govern the life of faith. In this case, those key moves were made by the two most recognizable Magisterial Reformers, Martin Luther and John Calvin, whose reactions against the Roman Catholic Church's handling of the doctrine of sanctification set the stage for four hundred years of Protestant engagement of the doctrine.

## The Reformation and Sanctification

The Reformers' insistence on *sola scriptura* (Scripture alone) significantly altered the doctrinal history of sanctification by returning to the biblical text as the authoritative source for the doctrine. Admittedly, the formulations of sanctification that influence the lives of Protestant Christians[1] are also shaped by other factors such as tradition, reason, and experience, functioning underneath Scripture as the controlling source.[2]

The Reformers protested how tradition had upstaged biblical authority in the Roman Catholicism of their day. Yet, even in subservience to Scripture, tradition and other factors still have been at work in the way different understandings of sanctification unfolded in the Reformation legacy. Each of the varied understandings of sanctification within Protestantism reflects the legacy of reaction against late-medieval Roman Catholic theology.[3] Leaders of the Magisterial Reformation were concerned about official church teaching and how that teaching affected people's lives as they understood it and

1. I have in view primarily the world of evangelical Protestantism, whether or not everyone would embrace the term "evangelical." The term is used with some ambivalence due to the unfortunate ways it has come to represent sociopolitical stances and, just as sadly, acquired a certain ethnic association. Still, I choose to use the term because it reflects the historic commitment to the *euangelion* (gospel, good news) and the essential tenets of historic orthodoxy that support that message, all the while acknowledging the current state of conflict and ambiguity surrounding the term. Though some, understandably, have chosen to abandon the term, I have to this point chosen to retain it and hope for its redemption. A well-reasoned case for its preservation and redemption is made by Young, "Recapturing Evangelical Identity and Mission." An appreciative, thorough, and comparative history of prominent traditions within Protestantism is offered by Buschart, *Exploring Protestant Traditions*. Members of the Roman Catholic and Eastern Orthodox traditions may see how their tradition could better contribute to or correct this conversation as it circulates within Protestantism. I can speak only from and to the Christian tradition(s) that I know best.

2. Albert Outler's "Quadrilateral," originally intended as a description of John Wesley's theological method, has been used diagnostically far beyond the Wesleyan tradition. See Outler, "The Wesleyan Quadrilateral." The Quadrilateral is not presented here as a definitive methodological framework, though it enjoys wide recognition and use. Even from within the Wesleyan tradition T. A. Noble points out that the Quadrilateral "is not exclusively Wesleyan and is not a quadrilateral!" Noble updates Outler's paradigm by suggesting four axioms that better reflect the basis for faithful theological reflection: Scripture, tradition, rational spiritual experience, and the "Trinitarian, Christocentric shape of Christian theology" (*Holy Trinity: Holy People*, 6–20).

3. This is not to ignore disputations about the nature of grace in the late Middle Ages—for example, the *via media* (middle way) and *via moderna* (modern way). Thanks to Andrew Hay for reminding me of this.

attempted to follow it.[4] From those reactions—those protestations—has come the dizzying panoply of teachings about sanctification that warrant ongoing examination.

A primary theological concern of the Reformers was the doctrine of justification, which Roman Catholic teaching had formulated so as to make justification essentially dependent on the exercise of free will and on some type of moral engagement as preparation to receive God's grace of justification. Thus, the exercise of free will was considered cooperative with God's grace, even though it resulted from God's infused and prevenient grace.[5] Sharing the key assumption that sanctification involves moral change, the Reformers saw an inappropriate connection between sanctification and justification—a connection that imposed impossible moral demands on people and compromised radical dependence on God's grace for salvation. The practical result "in the pew" was a debilitating moralism, relentless insecurity about one's status before God, and a dangerous presumption both about the extent of one's need for God's grace and about one's capacity to put oneself in a place to receive God's grace.

## Martin Luther

Martin Luther took the lead in this protest. As an Augustinian monk he had been immersed in Augustinian theology as it had been

4. A caveat is in order here. The "official" theology or doctrinal position of any ecclesiastical body on almost any topic seems never to be identical with how such positions are understood and practiced by those "in the pew." Thus, it could easily be argued that every ecclesiastical body or tradition has at least two theologies: an official or confessional theology, which is more or less codified, protected, and debated with sometimes excruciating nuance by the tradition's clergy and academics; and a functional or tacit theology, which is reflected in how those outside the clerical and academic ranks understand, process, and practice that doctrine in the complex, convoluted realities of their lives. This observation is intended to be more descriptive than critical. It is important because analysis of a tradition's functional, tacit theology may not align at every point with what the tradition's clergy and scholars affirm—and vice versa. Yet these formal, official theologies have tremendous impact as they are understood (or misunderstood) and shaped by innumerable other influences and find expression in the lives of a tradition's adherents. My analysis will focus on official doctrinal expressions, with sensitivity to the wider understanding, practice, and impact of those positions.

5. Thomas Aquinas, *Summa Theologica* II.113.7.

shaped by the Aristotelian constructs of the Scholastics. Luther's biographer James Mackinnon notes Peter Lombard, William of Ockham, and John Duns Scotus as Luther's "early mentors in the scholastic theology."[6] These figures, more Pelagian in their theological tendencies,[7] contributed to what Luther later described as his "torture of conscience,"[8] at the root of which was the question of the basis on which God is gracious to sinners.

Reflecting Thomas Aquinas's Aristotelian modes of thought, the Roman Catholic Church taught justification in a highly nuanced manner, which included the notion of infused grace along with intricate distinctions about the relation of infused grace to the activation of human free will.[9] Luther rejected the notion of infusion in his famous contention that justification is a single act of God to impute Christ's righteousness.

In the Counter-Reformation, the Council of Trent (1545–63) later solidified the church's stance in response to the Reformers' protests.

> Chapter VII In What the Justification of the Sinner Consists, and What Are Its Causes
>
> This disposition or preparation is followed by justification itself, which is not only a remission of sins but also the sanctification and renewal of the inward man through the voluntary reception of the grace and gifts whereby an unjust man becomes just and from being an enemy becomes a friend, that he may be an heir according to hope of life everlasting.[10]
>
> Canon 11 If anyone says that men are justified either by the sole imputation of the justice of Christ or by the sole remission of sins,

6. Mackinnon, *Luther and the Reformation*, 1:67.
7. That is, rejecting the notion of original sin or at least demurring with respect to the crippling effect of sin on the human will and thus attributing some capacity to the unredeemed human will to respond obediently to God.
8. Mackinnon, *Luther and the Reformation*, 1:78.
9. Thomas Aquinas, *Summa Theologica* II.113.7–10. Mackinnon points out that Luther had little direct acquaintance with Thomas and "wrongly . . . included Thomas Aquinas among the Pelagians of the Nominalist school who led him astray" (*Luther and the Reformation*, 1:78).
10. Schroeder, *Canons and Decrees*, 33.

> to the exclusion of the grace and the charity which is poured forth in their hearts by the Holy Ghost, and remains in them, or also that the grace by which we are justified is only the good will of God, let him be anathema.[11]

Trent's inclusion of the internal affections of grace and charity in the doctrine of justification represented what Luther and other Reformers considered the inappropriate and dangerous incorporation of sanctification into justification.

William Placher offers the following summary observations and comparison of Luther and Trent. For Luther, he says, "We are justified, though we remain sinners because God *imputes* Christ's righteousness to us. To be sure, in our lives as Christians we may turn gradually away from sin (this involves 'sanctification' and 'regeneration'), but that comes later and does not contribute to our justification, which derives not at all from our efforts."[12] For Trent, however,

> Grace comes first, an awakening and assisting grace that begins the process of justification, but people must consent to and cooperate with that grace. Justification, in turn, "is not only a remission of sins but also the sanctification and renewal of the inward man through the voluntary reception of the grace and gifts whereby an unjust man becomes just and from being an enemy becomes a friend." Luther had focused on an instant of justification, in which God saved sinners by pure grace but left them sinners—they were justified only because Christ's righteousness was imputed to them. Trent pictured justification as a process in which divine grace and human efforts cooperate at every step and not only lead God to count us as justified but also begin to transform us so that we more nearly deserve that status.[13]

For Luther, to subsume sanctification under justification in this particular manner and to attach justifying significance in any manner to personal transformation was seen as undermining the radical nature of God's grace for salvation.

11. Schroeder, *Canons and Decrees*, 43.
12. Placher, *History of Christian Theology*, 195 (emphasis original).
13. Placher, *History of Christian Theology*, 204.

Still, for Luther, "justification and 'sanctification' are extremely closely united,"[14] reflected perhaps in his insistence on *simul iustus et peccator* (simultaneously righteous and sinner), yet not in the same sense as he observed in Roman Catholic teaching. The key difference for Luther was that in justification Christ's righteousness is imputed to the believer and sanctification does not factor into that new standing before God. With that boundary in place, Luther went on to make sanctification part of what God does in the believer through faith. Commenting on Romans 6:19, he stated, "For through the terms 'sanctification' and 'cleanness' he [Paul] is trying to convey the same concept, namely, that the body should be pure, but not with just any kind of purity, but with that which comes from within, from the spirit of sanctifying faith. . . . Because through faith first the soul must be cleansed, so that in this way a holy soul can make the body clean for the sake of God; otherwise it would be a worthless chastity."[15] It is worth noting in his remark that he connected sanctification to cleansing but not necessarily to moral transformation. He offered a forthright description of sanctification in the third article of his *Small Catechism*:

> "I believe in the Holy Ghost; the holy Christian Church, the communion of saints; the forgiveness of sins; the resurrection of the body; and the life everlasting. Amen."
>
> What does this mean? I believe that I cannot by my own reason or strength believe in Jesus Christ, my Lord, or come to Him; but the Holy Ghost has called me by the Gospel, enlightened me with His gifts, sanctified and kept me in the true faith; even as He calls, gathers, enlightens, and sanctifies the whole Christian Church on earth, and keeps it with Jesus Christ in the one true faith; in which Christian Church He daily and richly forgives all sins to me and all believers, and will at the Last Day raise up me and all the dead, and give unto me and all believers in Christ eternal life.[16]

Later he elaborated:

14. Mannermaa, *Christ Present in Faith*, 54.
15. Luther, *Lectures on Romans*, 321.
16. Luther, *Small Catechism*, 11.

Q163. What is the work of the Holy Ghost? The Holy Ghost sanctifies me, that is, He *makes me holy*, by bringing me to faith in Christ and by imparting to me the blessings of redemption. (Sanctification in the wider sense includes everything that the Holy Ghost does in me.)[17]

Q169. What else has the Holy Ghost wrought in you by the Gospel? The Holy Ghost has *sanctified me in the true faith*, so that I can now overcome sin and *do good works*. (Sanctification in the narrower sense.)[18]

Notice in these statements how Luther connected sanctification to faith and saw it as the source for moral response. These features characterize subsequent Lutheran treatments of sanctification. Lutheran theologian Gerhard Forde relentlessly insists that any approach to sanctification veers into fruitless, if not dangerous, territory if it goes beyond deepening one's faith in the accomplished work of Christ.[19] Similarly, Helmut Thielicke states, "Sanctification is the process in which faith takes over all areas of life and sees its relevance for them."[20]

Thus, Luther's reaction against Roman Catholic teaching on justification congealed into a theology of sanctification that prioritized faith in Christ and the work of the Holy Spirit in sanctifying (purifying, making holy) through that faith. Luther certainly emphasized moral responsibility and action as a result of justification, though he did not appear to emphasize moral transformation in quite the same manner as what he perceived to be problematic in Roman Catholic doctrine. Though arguments from silence can be weak, the nuance of Luther's emphasis and lack of emphasis is crucial to understanding his contribution to the sanctification situation. It also sits in contrast to later, often Calvinistic, developments in the doctrine of sanctification that placed significant emphasis on moral progress or transformation as the progressive aspect of sanctification.

In his *Commentary on the Epistle to the Romans* (on 12:1–2), Luther emphasized the "living sacrifice" of our lives as "'holy,' that is, separated, detached, kept away from what is unclean, as something

17. Luther, *Small Catechism*, 125–26 (emphasis original).
18. Luther, *Small Catechism*, 129 (emphasis original).
19. Forde, "The Lutheran View."
20. Thielicke, *Evangelical Faith*, 1:107.

that is taken from some other use and set apart only for a use worthy of God. . . . Above all, it signifies the purity which we owe to God."[21] He went on to discuss the transformation and renewal that should result from this sacrifice and purity, but he did not directly equate transformation and renewal with holiness. Rather, in his view, the faith-generated sacrifice of our lives leads to holiness, which then leads to transformation and renewal.

Likewise, when he discussed the same text in *Lectures on Romans*, he never treated sanctification as synonymous with transformation but instead appeared to make transformation the result of the holy (sanctified) sacrifice of our lives to God.[22] This feature contrasts significantly with numerous later Protestant traditions for which Romans 12:1–2 became a hallmark text in support of progressive sanctification. For Luther, sanctification is not synonymous with transformation but rather leads to transformation.

Luther's understanding of sanctification can be summarized in the following points:

1. Sanctification results from faith, just as justification does.
2. Sanctification relates to personal cleansing from sin, while justification formally imputes Christ's righteousness to the believer.
3. Sanctification involves all that God does through the Holy Spirit to work out the fruit of redemption in a believer's life.
4. Sanctification applies to the church as well as to individual believers.

## John Calvin

John Calvin's concerns about the content and effects of Roman Catholic soteriology resembled Luther's, with the nature and the relationship of justification and sanctification as prominent concerns. Specifically, Calvin took issue with the notions of works as preparatory for the reception of justifying grace (contra Duns Scotus) and works of

21. Luther, *Epistle to the Romans*, 151.
22. Luther, *Lectures on Romans*, 435–36.

supererogation as compensation for deficiencies in our works (contra Bonaventura).[23] He contested Aquinas's emphasis that even though God's grace is the "principal cause" of our good works, our free will nonetheless serves as the meritorious instrument or means of good works.[24]

Though he affirmed Augustine in numerous respects, Calvin found problematic Augustine's subordination of grace to sanctification, because such a move implicitly places works ahead of grace.[25] Thus, he crystallized his view of justification: "Therefore, we explain justification simply as the acceptance with which God receives us into his favor as righteous men. And we say that it consists in the remission of sins and the imputation of Christ's righteousness."[26] Of particular note here is Calvin's somewhat tacit association of sanctification with works, to which we will return.

Like Luther, Calvin's view of the interface between justification and sanctification was shaped in part by his opposition to the teaching of Andreas Osiander (1498–1552), who resisted what he perceived to be overly legal connotations of justification understood as imputed righteousness. Calvin understood Osiander to argue instead that justification equated to actual, personal possession of Christ's righteousness—that is, righteousness within the believer's life and character. Calvin contended that this effectively "nullifies the certainty of salvation," insisting that, "because it is very well known by experience that the traces of sin always remain in the righteous, their justification must be very different from reformation into newness of life" (cf. Rom. 6:4).[27] Theologically, Calvin saw this move as an improper confusion of justification and regeneration.[28]

23. Calvin, *Institutes* 3.14.12.
24. Calvin, *Institutes* 3.15.7.
25. Calvin, *Institutes* 3.11.15.
26. Calvin, *Institutes* 3.11.2.
27. Calvin, *Institutes* 3.11.11. Ironically, Calvin goes on to insist that assurance of God's acceptance equates to a vigorous experience of faith, making assurance still seem elusive, though for different reasons than Osiander posited. Calvin states, "Scripture shows that God's promises are not established unless they are grasped with the full assurance of conscience. Wherever there is doubt or uncertainty, it pronounces them void" (3.13.4).
28. Calvin, *Institutes* 3.13.4; see editor's note 22.

Thus, Osiander provided a foil against which Calvin expressed his views on justification and sanctification. Each theme, for Calvin, was crucial in God's overall work of salvation, though each deals with a specific and distinct type of righteousness. Two statements distill his thinking on this point.

> For Paul's statement is not redundant: that Christ was given to us for our righteousness and sanctification [I Cor. 1:30]. And whenever he reasons—from the salvation purchased for us, from God's fatherly love, and from Christ's grace—that we are called to holiness and cleanness, he clearly indicates that to be justified means something different from being made new creatures.[29]

> In short, whoever wraps up two kinds of righteousness in order that miserable souls may not repose wholly in God's mere mercy, crowns Christ in mockery with a wreath of thorns [Mark 15:17, etc.].[30]

Calvin insisted that justification before God comes as a free act of God's grace, accepted only and entirely by faith. As such it does not change a person's character. Yet, by virtue of establishing a relationship with God, justification effects through the Holy Spirit a real union with Christ that sets in motion a lifelong process of growth and change. Thus, Calvin's view of sanctification emerges.

For Calvin, justification and sanctification are still integrally linked, though in a delicately nuanced manner. Those nuances deserve careful attention, since he spoke of the "beginning" and "progress" of justification,[31] which can sound strangely similar to aspects of the Roman Catholic teaching that he so fiercely rejected. The following extended passage captures his understanding of that integration.

> Why, then, are we justified by faith? Because by faith we grasp Christ's righteousness, by which alone we are reconciled to God. Yet you could not grasp this without at the same time grasping sanctification also. For he "is given unto us for righteousness, wisdom, sanctification, and redemption" [I Cor. 1:30]. Therefore Christ justifies no one whom he

29. Calvin, *Institutes* 3.11.6 (brackets original).
30. Calvin, *Institutes* 3.11.12 (brackets original).
31. Calvin, *Institutes* 3.14.1.

does not at the same time sanctify. These benefits are joined together by an everlasting and indissoluble bond, so that those whom he illumines by his wisdom, he redeems; those whom he redeems, he justifies; those whom he justifies, he sanctifies.

But, since the question concerns only righteousness and sanctification, let us dwell upon these. Although we may distinguish them, Christ contains both of them inseparably in himself. Do you wish, then, to attain righteousness in Christ? You must first possess Christ; but you cannot possess him without being made partaker in his sanctification, because he cannot be divided into pieces [I Cor. 1:13]. Since, therefore, it is solely by expending himself that the Lord gives us these benefits to enjoy, he bestows both of them at the same time, the one never without the other. Thus it is clear how true it is that we are justified not without works yet not through works, since in our sharing in Christ, which justifies us, sanctification is just as much included as righteousness.[32]

Thus, Calvin relocated sanctification and justification from the believer (as spiritual possessions or features) to Christ, who indwells the believer and with whom the believer is united through faith. Only through this faith-based indwelling do good works appear, and through this indwelling they will necessarily and inevitably appear.

Calvin's understanding of sanctification can be summarized in the following points:

1. Justification involves sanctification as the experiential outworking of Christ's righteousness bestowed (imputed) in justification.
2. Sanctification is rooted in communion with Christ that, while instrumentally resulting from faith, essentially comes through the agency of the Holy Spirit.
3. Sanctification produces the fruit of life intrinsic to the righteousness of Christ bestowed (imputed) through faith.
4. Sanctification demands and involves purity of life, the mortification of the flesh and its lusts, and the formation of the heart to obey God's law.[33]

32. Calvin, *Institutes* 3.16.1 (brackets original).
33. Calvin, *Institutes* 3.14.9.

5. Sanctification by the Spirit empowers and leads to the cultivation of this purity of life.[34]

The fourth and fifth points provide the basis for suggesting that even though Calvin did associate sanctification with transformation, he also saw sanctification as the basis for transformation. That basis, which constitutes the focus of this book, played a far more influential role in Calvin's understanding of sanctification than it has in many subsequent Calvinistic framings of the doctrine through the years. Calvin saw the accomplished aspect of sanctification as tightly linked to union with Christ through the Holy Spirit and as absolutely central to everything else about sanctification. He states, "Faith rests upon the knowledge of Christ. And Christ cannot be known apart from the sanctification of his Spirit."[35] His emphases set up our next set of considerations because the careful nuances of his position have not always been well preserved.

## Conclusion

We can hardly overestimate the formative influence of Luther and Calvin on the current doctrine(s) of sanctification that frame and direct the lives of contemporary Christians who live somewhere in the legacy of the Reformation. These two Reformers sought to correct what they saw as seriously problematic formulations of sanctification in the medieval Roman Catholic Church. In part, they did this by insisting that sanctification and other biblical doctrines be both properly distinguished and properly related. In doing so, they brought to the surface key themes such as faith, the role of the Spirit, and union with Christ that had been ignored, obscured, or simply undeveloped in relation to sanctification. For this we are in their debt.

Their work, of course, was not perfect and did not close the conversation for all time. Theological reflection on God's revelation does

34. Calvin, *Institutes* 3.11.1. This is the second part of Calvin's famous *duplex gratia* (double grace), the first part relating to justification: "being reconciled to God through Christ's blamelessness, we may have in heaven instead of a Judge a gracious Father."

35. Calvin, *Institutes* 3.2.8.

not work that way. It must be noted that, despite the protests they put forward, they assumed to varying extents the moral understanding of sanctification that they inherited from late-medieval Roman Catholicism, the significance of which must not be overlooked. Theological positions are always and profoundly shaped by that to which they react. Yet, thankfully, they moved the line of scrimmage forward significantly. Subsequent years saw their emphases modified, codified, and circulated. In some cases codifications became calcifications. In other cases modifications became improvisations. Consistently, however, the initial and subsequent expressions of the doctrine of sanctification have been placed in dialogue with the realities of the faith journey in the lives of real people who for a wide array of reasons have not uniformly experienced those doctrinal expressions as healthy or helpful. Our exploration of how we got to where we are must now turn to some of the more influential ventures—the modifications—in that doctrinal history.

# 2

# New Ventures in Sanctification

The post-Reformation theological tradition reflects a checkered history for the doctrine of sanctification. Debates swirl about the most appropriate way to understand sanctification within the comprehensive context of biblical revelation and, more specifically, how to understand its relationship to justification and other aspects of God's redemptive work. The pattern of emphases within Protestant evangelical traditions reflects Reformation reactions against late-medieval Roman Catholicism's configuration of sanctification in relation to justification. Since Hebrews 12:14 makes the striking reference to "holiness without which no one will see the Lord," the stakes are high. Sanctification is neither ancillary nor optional for the Christian life.

Appreciation of the current "sanctification situation" depends on a closer look at the impact of four centuries of Reformation-influenced developments and permutations in this doctrine. Theologians may insist that how people respond to doctrines is irrelevant to whether those doctrines are true. In one sense that is correct. Yet the patterns of how doctrines actually impact God's people are not to be ignored as a diagnostic for scholarly formulations that can otherwise seem true in the safe confines of a library while untested in life.

Actual Christian living amplifies the implications of nuances that scholars articulate within a doctrine. Experience does not determine truth, but it can provide clarification and validation for theological claims. Thus, a review of this doctrine's history and residual impact will provide clues for the type of midcourse corrections and recalibrations needed.

## Lutheran Expressions

Martin Luther's theology was expressed confessionally in the Augsburg Confession (1530) and formalized in the Formula of Concord (1577). The Augsburg Confession elaborates the Lutheran position on justification but does not explicitly develop a doctrine of sanctification. Rather, what is generally labeled as sanctification is described as the relation of good works to the renewal brought about by the Holy Spirit. It states,

> Our teachers teach . . . that it is necessary to do good works, not that we should trust to merit grace by them but because it is the will of God. It is only by faith that forgiveness of sins and grace are apprehended, and because through faith the Holy Spirit is received, hearts are so renewed and endowed with new affections as to be able to bring forth good works.[1]

The Formula of Concord more directly articulates the relationship between justification and sanctification.

> That neither renewal, sanctification, virtues, nor other good works are our righteousness before God, nor are they to be made and posited to be a part or a cause of our justification, nor under any kind of pretense, title, or name are they to be mingled with the article of justification as pertinent or necessary to it. The righteousness of faith consists solely in the forgiveness of sins by sheer grace, entirely for the sake of Christ's merit, which treasures are offered to us in the promise of the Gospel and received, accepted, applied to us, and made our own solely through faith.
>
> In this way, too, the proper order between faith and good works is bound to be maintained and preserved, as well as between justification and renewal or sanctification. . . . After the person is justified,

1. Grane, "The Augsburg Confession, Art. 20," in *Augsburg Confession*, 197.

> the Holy Spirit next renews and sanctifies him, and from this renewal and sanctification the fruits of good works will follow. This is not to be understood, however, as though justification and sanctification are separated from each other in such a way as though on occasion true faith could coexist and survive for a while side by side with a wicked intention, but this merely shows the order in which one thing precedes or follows the other. . . .
>
> That righteousness by faith before God consists of two pieces or parts, namely, the gracious forgiveness of sins and, as a second element, renewal or sanctification.[2]

Several key themes mark these Lutheran formulations. First is the insistence that justification and sanctification both involve faith but in different ways and to different ends. By faith we receive justification that results in forgiveness. By faith we also receive the Holy Spirit, who prompts us toward good works. Second, justification and sanctification must be kept logically distinct. Justification has to do with a righteousness that determines our acceptance before God and comes from God only by grace, while sanctification has to do with the Holy Spirit's renewal that expresses this righteousness in good works. Acceptance before God can never be confused with or based on good works. Third, sanctification is subsequent to justification, and, because of the renewal it involves, good works will follow.

## Calvinistic Expressions

John Calvin's sanctification emphases were codified in two dominant streams that drew on his theology. The Heidelberg Catechism guided the Reformed church on the European continent, while the Westminster Confession did the same for English Calvinism in the Presbyterian church.

From the Westminster Larger Catechism:

> Question 75: What is sanctification?
>
> Answer: Sanctification is a work of God's grace, whereby they whom God has, before the foundation of the world, chosen to be holy,

2. "Formula of Concord," in Tappert, *Book of Concord*, 546, 548.

> are in time, through the powerful operation of His Spirit applying the death and resurrection of Christ unto them, renewed in their whole man after the image of God; having the seeds of repentance unto life, and all other saving graces, put into their hearts, and those graces so stirred up, increased, and strengthened, as that they more and more die unto sin, and rise unto newness of life.[3]

Chapter 13 of the Westminster Standards provides an extended explanation of this answer, including relevant biblical passages. Two features of that explanation warrant attention. First, the Standards cite multiple passages that highlight various aspects of Christ's redemptive work on our behalf yet do not actually refer to sanctification.[4] This models a questionable tendency found in a variety of subsequent doctrinal treatments of sanctification: to build the doctrine on passages that do not talk about sanctification. While we cannot limit the doctrine only to those texts that use the word and should not assume that other passages have no relevance to sanctification,[5] this move in the Standards represents a widespread and problematic disproportioning of the doctrine that diminishes the role of its dominant motif (what sanctification accomplishes) and inflates the role of its iterative motif (what sanctification demands and produces).

Second, numerous biblical texts that refer to sanctification are taken to equate sanctification with subjective renewal.[6] To question this practice does not ignore the biblical emphasis on subjective renewal/growth or support "instantaneous" versions of sanctification as moral completion. It is simply to question the assumption that sanctification and transformation are synonymous and the tendency to allow transformation to dominate considerations of sanctification.

The Standards recognize that the accomplished ("positional") aspect of sanctification, rooted in regeneration, constitutes the basis or

3. Bordwine, *Guide to the Westminster Confession*, 318–19.

4. For example, Rom. 6:6; Phil. 3:10.

5. While numerous texts that do not specifically refer to sanctification are used to support the notion of sanctification as transformation (e.g., Rom. 12:2), this does not make those texts irrelevant to sanctification. However, this type of usage prompts review of whether such a doctrinal construction best represents the overall biblical contours and ethos of the concept.

6. For example, John 17:17; Eph. 5:26.

source for believers to be "further sanctified, really and personally."[7] However, the language in that phrase—"further sanctified, really"—suggests that sanctification, as such, exists on a sort of sliding scale. This is an assumption that a thorough, canonical examination of the texts does not substantiate, as we will see in chapters 3 and 4. Moreover, this language charts the course for the pattern in which sanctification as accomplished is minimally emphasized and sanctification as growth and transformation in Christlikeness is predominantly emphasized.

## Post-Reformation Iterations and Permutations

Subsequent variations on the sanctification themes developed by Luther and Calvin bring to mind the apostle John's closing description of Jesus's ministry: "If every one of them [his works] were written down, I suppose that the world itself could not contain the books that would be written" (John 21:25). At the risk of doing injustice to those variations, brief descriptions of two highly influential variations will help clarify some features of the current sanctification situation.

### *John Wesley*

John Wesley left one of the most notable imprints on Protestant views of sanctification. As any reader of Wesley knows and as Wesley scholars readily admit, he was not a systematic theologian. His theological conclusions were forged in the crucible of itinerant preaching and wide-ranging pastoral involvement in people's lives. Hence, Wesley was not as concerned with a theological system marked by tight, demonstrable consistency that would withstand analytical scrutiny. He was not bound to the canons of scholasticism, either Roman Catholic or Protestant, and was driven more by concern for the gospel's accessibility and immediate impact on people's lives.[8]

7. Bordwine, *Guide to the Westminster Confession*, 75.

8. Noble, *Holy Trinity: Holy People*, 99–100. Noble clarifies how Wesley, as a product of his time period, both did and did not utilize features of a scholastic approach. He thought in doctrinal categories defined by the Thirty-Nine Articles of the Church of England but "was more shaped by the narratives and practicalities

Wesley drew on and sometimes fused theological sources from both the Western/Latin tradition (e.g., sin resulting in guilt) and the Eastern/Greek tradition (e.g., sin resulting in disease of the soul).[9] Informed also by his own experience of the Christian journey, Wesley saw justification in a less formal or positional manner and blended it with the personal, existential experience of forgiveness. Randy Maddox points out that "Wesley always understood Divine grace to convey both *pardon* and *power*."[10] Thus, he was uncomfortable with the type of distinction that some Reformers made between justification and sanctification.

Yet, in order to avoid the moralistic hazards of Roman Catholicism, "he distinguished between our initial justification, which is *not* dependent on prior holiness of life, and our final justification, which *is* dependent upon our justifying faith bearing fruit in sanctification."[11] Maddox points out that "while he highly valued God's justifying grace, Wesley did not allow justification to dominate his understanding of salvation to the degree that is common among so many Western Christians, particularly Protestants. For him the greatest value of justification was precisely its contribution to the higher goal of sanctification—our recovery of the Likeness of God."[12]

Sanctification, for Wesley, was marked by the command and the possibility of "entire sanctification." Paul's prayer in 1 Thessalonians 5:23 that believers would be sanctified "entirely" (implying a scale of sorts) served as the basis for his assertion that believers could actually be so thoroughly motivated by the love and grace of God as to be pure in heart during the course of this life. He claims, "[Firstly,] a Christian is so far perfect as not to commit sin. . . . It is only of grown Christians it can be affirmed they are in such a sense perfect, as, secondly, to be freed from evil thoughts and evil tempers."[13] Even more pointedly he remarks, "This it is to be a perfect man, to be

of Scripture than by the dry, scholastic, systematic structure found in seventeenth-century theologians like Arminius or John Owen" (100).

9. Maddox, *Responsible Grace*, 73.

10. Maddox, *Responsible Grace*, 168 (emphasis original).

11. Maddox, *Responsible Grace*, 169 (emphasis original).

12. Maddox, *Responsible Grace*, 172.

13. Wesley, *Christian Perfection*, 19.

'sanctified throughout'; even 'to have a heart so all-flaming with the love of God.'"[14] Further, "Scripture perfection is pure love, filling the heart, and governing all the words and action."[15]

Lest his view of sanctification be reduced to nothing more than this grand vision, it must also be noted that Wesley was fond of using the phrase "growth in grace,"[16] an emphasis often overlooked in his approach to sanctification. William Greathouse observes that Wesley saw sanctification as initiated by justification when the seed of holiness is sown, though that seed of sin remains until the believer is sanctified entirely. Thus, he states, "For Wesley, sanctification in this initial sense is the ethical counterpart of justification."[17]

The Wesleyan tradition, in its numerous variations, occupies a prominent place within what has come to be known as the "Holiness Movement" or "Holiness Traditions." Wesley's theology of sanctification—including how he related sanctification to justification—certainly intensified the focus on personal purity. T. A. Noble reminds us that Wesley's doctrine of sanctification has in numerous cases been made into something more or different than Wesley himself taught. Other "holiness" movements have blended aspects of Wesley's thought with idiosyncratic biblical interpretations and cultural practices in ways that caricature Wesley's actually teaching on sanctification.[18]

Despite the fact that in many cases Wesley's teaching on sanctification led to versions of piety that bordered on individualistic narcissism, Wesley himself exercised keen awareness of social engagement. His insistence that sanctification is measured by love points to this emphasis on social responsibility. Notwithstanding Wesley's modifications of the doctrine of sanctification, he carried forward the dominant emphasis on sanctification as subjective renewal, with the net effects of reinforcing the association of sanctification with transformation and of fostering an inwardly focused set of metrics for the sanctified life.

14. Wesley, *Christian Perfection*, 30. Here Wesley is quoting from Archbishop Usher.

15. Wesley, *Christian Perfection*, 51.

16. Wesley, *Christian Perfection*, 98.

17. Greathouse, *From the Apostles to Wesley*, 14.

18. Noble, *Holy Trinity: Holy People*, 74.

### *The Keswick Movement*

Within the broader evangelical world in Great Britain and the United States, the doctrine of sanctification also displays the imprint of the Keswick movement, which has adopted—in some ways blended—select emphases from the Lutheran, Calvinistic, and Wesleyan traditions. The early Keswick movement sought in part to rectify what were perceived as problems in the sanctification doctrines of other traditions. Often those supposed errors and deficiencies were understood to breed unnecessary difficulty and discouragement as people navigated the life of faith.

In the late nineteenth century, Hannah Whitall Smith helped give this unique interpretation of sanctification widespread influence through annual conferences in Keswick, England. In her spiritual autobiography, she chronicled her personal spiritual journey from a life of relentless, disheartening struggle to please God to a life of freedom before God simply by surrendering fully to God through faith.[19]

In the mid-twentieth century, Steven Barabas offered a more thorough exposition of the Keswick movement's theological underpinnings, particularly its insistence on sanctification by faith. Through dependence on the Holy Spirit, faith is understood to counteract the power of the sin nature and allows the believer to live in a place of spiritual rest and victory.[20] Barabas points out, "Keswick tells us that one of the principal reasons for this [widespread sense of] failure and defeat on the part of earnest Christians is found in wrong, unscriptural ways of seeking sanctification."[21]

Keswick incorporates the Lutheran emphasis on faith, yet it focuses far more on the process and subjective nature of sanctification than does the Lutheran tradition. It agrees with the Calvinistic tradition about the ongoing presence and influence of the sin nature but rejects the notion that sanctification should be a struggle. It reflects the punctiliar expectations of sanctification found in the Wesleyan

19. H. W. Smith, *The Christian's Secret of a Happy Life*, 68.

20. Barabas, *So Great Salvation*, 84–98.

21. Barabas, *So Great Salvation*, 69. Barabas claims that among these "wrong ways of seeking sanctification" are the assumptions that sanctification (1) is automatic, (2) is "a matter of gradual growth," (3) eradicates the "sin principle," or (4) simply suppresses the old nature (69–75).

tradition yet insists that a sanctified life of freedom from struggle is far more accessible and normative for all Christians.

Teachings of the English Keswick movement fostered the "Victorious Life movement in America."[22] Keswick spirituality has, arguably, wielded more widespread influence on mainstream evangelicalism in North America than any other distinct understanding of sanctification. Its theologically eclectic nature merged, unofficially, with dispensational theology and various other social factors to give it traction and a lingering influence in countless congregations and other circles to this day.[23]

Spirited interaction between proponents of Keswick spirituality and, particularly, those of Calvinistic persuasion has highlighted the question of "how" sanctification occurs in the daily experience of believers. More specifically, the question involves the role of faith in relation to human effort in sanctification and the nature of growth in Christlikeness (understood as sanctification). These questions have received considerable attention on the assumption that they are the proper questions to ask. As students of theological method know, theological answers are only as good as the questions asked. We must question our questions, in this case examining whether the focal points of discussion about sanctification best represent the way the doctrine is presented in Scripture. To that task we will turn in part 2.

## Residual Effects of Sanctification Doctrines

Efforts to correct and refine the doctrine of sanctification began early in the wake of the Reformation and have continued through the present day, suggesting that the nuanced doctrinal reconfigurations of Luther and Calvin, however helpful, did not resolve the matter. Efforts such as the Keswick movement were not anchored in any one tradition's understanding of sanctification but reacted against various emphases in particular Reformation streams while drawing on other emphases in those same streams. Other correctives have emerged from within different Reformation traditions and have sought to clarify as well as correct.

22. Barabas, *So Great Salvation*, 71.

23. For analysis of this phenomenon, see Marsden, *Fundamentalism and American Culture*, 79; Payne, *Theology of the Christian Life in J. I. Packer's Thought*, 33–36, 147.

From within Dutch Calvinism in 1952, G. C. Berkouwer commented on widespread confusion over whether sanctification is simply a Christian way of expressing the concern for morality found within the public sector, denoting nothing substantially distinct, or whether it refers to an idiosyncratic and psychological domain of life that is isolated from other concerns.[24] Berkouwer also expressed concern that Protestant Christians were still plagued by lack of clarity about the relationship between justification and sanctification, and the role of God's grace and human faith in those motifs.[25]

The struggle over sanctification—these residual effects of the Reformation—includes but extends beyond these carefully measured and nuanced theological discussions. It marks the lives of all serious Christians in some manner. This conflict has roots in the soil of deeply existential and personal struggle, which wields considerable influence on the biblical and theological reflections that take place.

One curious example of the interplay between personal experience and theological reflection on the doctrine of sanctification is found in the contrasting journeys of Hannah Whitall Smith and J. I. Packer. Smith's embrace of Keswick spirituality was born of desperation and exasperation with the Calvinistic insistence on spiritual struggle and human responsibility. In moving away from that, she found liberation in an entirely faith-based approach to sanctification. In contrast, well-known theologian J. I. Packer, after experiencing a Christian awakening as an Oxford undergraduate, was discipled in Keswick spirituality by the Oxford Intercollegiate Christian Union. However, his experience of that sanctification model led him to a place of introspective despair, ever unsure whether he had identified and surrendered everything that might impede the victorious Christian life. While serving as a librarian for Latimer House, a Puritan study center in Oxford, Packer came across John Owen's writings and found in them a liberatingly realistic account of the Christian life as a Spirit-empowered, lifelong struggle against sin and temptation.[26]

24. Berkouwer, *Faith and Sanctification*, 12.

25. Berkouwer, *Faith and Sanctification*, 17–22.

26. McGrath, *To Know and Serve God*, 22–25. This was corroborated in a personal correspondence from Packer to me on July 17, 2000. See also his theological

Contrasts such as these illustrate the confusion and complexity surrounding the question of what it means to be sanctified. Even when different parties affirm God's role as primary and human faith as secondary, questions continually emerge about the specific complexion of that interface, the nature of faith, the Holy Spirit's role, and experiential expectations. These concerns continue to dominate the discussion and drive us back to questions about the contours of the biblical profile of sanctification.

Those who work in discipleship and other formational ministries deal routinely with Christians who take seriously the call to grow in Christlikeness and yet who are burdened with guilt over their cycles of struggle and their perceived lack of progress. Exhortations about "transformed lives" portray the possibility of radical change that can initially motivate and inspire but can just as quickly dishearten and disillusion if continual struggle occurs. Metrics by which substantive growth can be assessed seem opaque and elusive. The actual (not theoretical) pursuit of growth in Christlikeness is often quietly crippled by expectations that outweigh resources and by models of the Christian life that polarize restful trust in God against the normalization of struggle and weariness.

All of this takes place in the name of sanctification. When sanctification is assumed to be primarily something out in front of the believer, something yet to be attained, something that results from a psychologically subtle interface between trusting God in just the right manner and engaging the right type of disciplines and __________ (fill in the blank), the acceptability and fulfillment of our lives before God ends up as a nice theological affirmation that bears little resemblance to practical, daily experience.

## Conclusion

The primary sanctification clarifications offered by the Magisterial Reformers straightened and repaved what had become dead-end or dangerous theological roadways. Subsequent sanctification efforts ran

---

critique of the Keswick movement: Packer, "'Keswick' and the Reformed Doctrine of Sanctification."

along these paths, sometimes widening them and sometimes overlapping them. Yet, the pattern of continued struggle and confusion suggests that deeper groundwork is needed in order to avoid sinkholes and move these paths forward.

Developments and refinements in the doctrine of sanctification can never be isolated from the lived experience of God's people. The ebb and flow of attention to sanctification within scholarly circles and beyond has failed to bring about substantive consensus or resolution. In the relentless biblical and theological ping-pong[27] about sanctification, a core question seems never to have been put to rest: What actually constitutes sanctification? The answer to this question may seem rather obvious in light of the vast lexical and textual work that has been done. Yet experiential as well as theological dilemmas remain, which suggests that additional work is needed.

In more recent years publishers have invited scholars from different Protestant traditions into conversation with one another, both to summarize their respective tradition's understanding of sanctification and to critique the others.[28] This work has been productive, yet continued progress necessitates further clarification of key terms and a narrowing of the conversation to make sure that competing views are actually talking about the same thing in the same sense.

Thus, in the next section we will turn to a reexamination of key biblical texts on which the biblical doctrine of sanctification is based, looking for what is and is not actually said, as well as the underlying and overarching pattern that emerges in those texts. Just as important, we will hold up into the light of God's Word assumptions about sanctification that may not have been adequately scrutinized and perhaps have been asked to hold more weight than they can bear.

27. I borrowed this phrase from Mitchell, *How to Play Theological Ping-Pong*, 166. However, I must admit to adapting the phrase to depict something a bit different than what Mitchell had in view.

28. See Dieter et al., *Five Views on Sanctification*; Alexander, *Christian Spirituality*.

PART TWO

# The Biblical Story Line Revisited

# 3

# A Potent Backstory

## *Consecration in the Old Testament*

Both scholarly and popular treatments of sanctification acknowledge its roots in the Old Testament concept of "consecration."[1] The *qādôš* (קדש) word group in Hebrew supports and describes the Old Testament concept of holiness. Though the connection between the consecration noun (*qādôš*) in the Old Testament and the sanctification adjective (*hagios*, ἅγιος) in the New Testament is frequently recognized, the Old Testament root needs further examination in order to see what it implies for sanctification in the New Testament.[2] The power of sanctification in the lives of God's people now can best be understood in light of what consecration meant and how it functioned in people's lives then.

1. For examples of this from authors who have wielded widespread influence on their traditions, see Chafer, *He That Is Spiritual*, 106–7; Greathouse, *From the Apostles to Wesley*, 19–24.

2. Some of the long-standing confusion and debate about consecration/sanctification may have derived in part from ambiguity about how the relevant terms function in Hebrew and Greek (and even Latin, e.g., *sanctus*); how they are translated into English, especially in their verbal forms; and whether transitive or intransitive connotations are intended.

Clearly, God called Israel to be a holy people. They were unilaterally chosen and set apart by God as God's instrument for the redemptive blessing of the world (Gen. 12:2–3) and consecrated to the Lord (Exod. 19:6) for that purpose. This consecration was accomplished—at least instrumentally—and expressed through rituals in which the people consecrated themselves in response to God having first consecrated them. The purification involved in consecration prepared them to meet the Lord—to come close to God's presence—and is a salient feature that will resurface.

The "uncleanness" from which the people had to be purified referred in part to any moral impurities or sins they had committed. As the prophets later showed, the ethical dimension of their lives was often the object of God's judgment, particularly in relation to their unfaithfulness to God's covenant. Yet, purification also referred to perfectly acceptable, even honorable aspects of life such as sexual relations, which had no intrinsically negative moral or ethical connotations but rather represented the normal and mundane. Approaching the presence of the Living God was never to be considered mundane or ordinary. God's presence was always to be considered (because it actually is) life-altering—life-giving, life-sustaining, and sometimes life-ending—because God is the Holy One.[3]

All other features and dimensions of consecration in the Old Testament must be seen in light of the obvious fact that God's decisive consecration of Israel preceded and defined their responsive acts of consecration. The significance of this sequence can be obscured by preoccupation with the experiential character of consecration (and later of sanctification)—that is, the human response, expressions, and results. God set the nation of Israel apart and made the nation holy prior to their existence as distinct persons. That feature sets the pace for several assertions that will be developed throughout this book.

3. Peter Gentry challenges the widely held notion that *qādôš* (holy) refers to being set apart in the sense of separation. Rather, he argues, it means to be "consecrated, devoted, or prepared for the meeting of God and man" ("The Meaning of 'Holy,'" 404). Gentry contends that *qādôš*, even in relation to God's holiness, refers not to transcendence or otherness but to God's faithful devotion to God's people and to God's purposes for and through them (411–13).

Whatever holiness involves experientially—however it is expressed in specific choices and practices for individuals and communities—those experiential aspects are made possible by the prior act of God to make people holy. Only because God's people have already been made holy by God can they experience that holiness, though the nature of experiential holiness is yet to be reexamined and should not be presumed. God's act of consecration defined who they were. And their identity was far more than a formal construct or something merely "positional." They were brought into a particular, covenantal, and purpose-laden relationship with the Living God.

For God to make covenant with Israel was to place God's self in active—not passive—relationship to them. That relationship involved the creation and gift of a legal structure to direct and preserve their corporate life. It involved an identity that would distinguish them from all other nations or people groups. In covenant relationship with them, God provided for their corporate life specific guidance, protection, provision, and obligations. As a consequence, their consecration made possible and obligatory their formation. Israel had to grow into the character of people God had made them to be—consecrated people invited into God's presence to share in God's holiness.

## Definitive Consecration Vignettes

The theme of consecration runs throughout the Old Testament but appears most definitively in the Pentateuch. The *qādôš* word group is typically understood to convey the sense of "apartness, sacredness."[4] Select examples will suffice to demonstrate the powerful character of this divine act and how it relates to human experience.

### *Genesis 2:3*

So God blessed the seventh day and hallowed it, because on it God rested from all the work that he had done in creation.

4. Brown, Driver, and Briggs, "קדשׁ," 871.

The verbal form of *qādôš* appears here to denote God's setting apart of the seventh day. This divine act, including God's own rest at the conclusion of creation, forms the basis for the later Sabbath commands. Interestingly, the first focal point of holiness mentioned in Scripture is not a person but a day. The holiness of the seventh day was purposeful—rest—which later became ritualized in Israel's cultus as the day of worship and rest. The holy day was a day for particular types of engagement with God and response to God.

#### *Exodus 3:1–6*[5]

Moses's encounter with God at the burning bush provides a paradigmatic example of holiness. This scenario centers on the revealed presence of God, which defines everything else that happens. Moses was summoned to the bush, yet God gave him two noteworthy warnings: "Come no closer" and "Remove the sandals from your feet." The ground on which Moses stood in front of the bush was holy. Peter Gentry argues that *qōdeš* in this text refers not to any intrinsic feature or character of the mountain (3:1) or of the ground itself on which Moses stood but to the fact that God was present there.[6]

Both divine warnings portray the significance and power of God's presence. The second deserves particular attention because, like the Sabbath, the object of consecration was inanimate and otherwise utterly ordinary. This particular patch of dirt was holy because it was in certain proximity to the revealed presence of God and because it occasioned interaction with God. The removal of Moses's sandals, Carol Meyers points out, indicated customary respect in that culture.[7] Doing so was part of the necessary preparation for being in God's presence—a theme developed in more detail in subsequent consecration accounts as both priests and people were required to make particular preparations for approaching and communing with God at various proximities. The closer one came to God, the more elaborate were the preparations—a point with more explicitly developed

5. For the sake of space, some longer texts have not been reproduced.
6. Gentry, "The Meaning of 'Holy,'" 403.
7. Meyers, *Exodus*, 53.

theological implications in the New Testament and with significance for all people. Interestingly, Moses himself is never referred to as holy in this account. Yet holiness was central to what transpired. It was a holy place and a holy moment.

As subsequent consecration episodes demonstrate, consecration always involved, at least implicitly, God's covenantal presence, commitment, participation, and externally focused purposes for the consecrated people. Furthermore, and perhaps proleptically, transformation resulted from the consecration event without being synonymous with it. Brevard Childs marks this holy encounter as a transformative event in Moses's life: "The old life of shepherding was ended; the new life of deliverer was beginning."[8] By the holiness of this event Moses was called and empowered by God.

### *Exodus 13:1–2*

> The Lord said to Moses: "Consecrate to me all the firstborn; whatever is the first to open the womb among the Israelites, of human beings and of animals, is mine."

Immediately after delivering Israel from 430 years in Egypt, God installed the Passover and claimed every firstborn male, both human and animal. Meyers points out the ironic significance of the consecration of firstborn males to God, in contrast to Pharaoh's edict to kill all firstborn Israelite children. Instead, God claimed them and redeemed them.[9] James Bruckner interprets this as indicating God's protection and value of the firstborn.[10]

This divine act of consecration expressed God's protective and purposeful concern for Israel, though that may be easy to miss when looking only at the formal imperative. Implicit in consecration was God's personal commitment to those who were consecrated. At times God's commands to consecrate may sound harsh to modern ears, yet behind this rigor laid God's commitment to protect Israel and keep moving them forward in their divinely appointed purposes. All

8. Childs, *Book of Exodus*, 72.
9. Meyers, *Exodus*, 102–3.
10. Bruckner, *Exodus*, 123.

imperatives related to consecration were propelled by the grace of God's covenantal election and commitment.

#### *Exodus 19:10–11*

> The LORD said to Moses: "Go to the people and consecrate them today and tomorrow. Have them wash their clothes and prepare for the third day, because on the third day the LORD will come down upon Mount Sinai in the sight of all the people."

This account depicts the implications of consecration. Moses met with God at Mount Sinai, where God's covenant commitment and expectations were reiterated (19:3–6). He returned to the people of Israel with God's message, to which they responded with their vow of obedience to the covenant (19:7–8). God then summoned the people to the foot of Mount Sinai, where they could hear God interacting with Moses and learn to trust Moses as their divinely appointed leader. Yet, God instructed Moses to consecrate the people before they could approach the mountain. This consecration ritual of washing their clothes and abstaining from sexual relations (v. 15), along with a boundary they were not to cross, preserved them from the threat of death that would occur by coming too close to God at the mountain.[11]

Douglas Stuart notes that it may have been quite an undertaking for everyone in Israel to wash their clothes in two days, since they did not wash their clothes as often as modern people do and the available water was prioritized for people and animals to drink. The command symbolized God's intolerance for impurity and was intended to prepare the entire nation for this "special covenantal encounter with Yahweh."[12] This was a decidedly relational act on God's part,

11. Gentry, "The Meaning of 'Holy,'" 406. Gentry notes that this restriction was "given for a precise reason. In 'not coming near' their wives, the Israelites are ready 'to come near' God. God wants to prepare the people for a very special meeting." Gentry also observes, regarding the fact that Moses was commanded to consecrate the people, "At this point the notion of 'sanctification' is overcharged with a moral sense in many expositions. Such a meaning cannot be justified here by reason of the context" (405).

12. Stuart, *Exodus*, 428. Stuart also notes that the command to abstain from sexual relations pointed to the importance of avoiding anything that would distract attention from the significance of the encounter with God (425–26).

though not relational in the sense in which that term is often used in contemporary Western culture. Gentry clarifies that "Israel as a nation קדוש is a nation given access to the presence of Yahweh and devoted solely to the service and worship of the Lord."[13]

The restrictions and warnings against people coming too close to the mountain signaled God's inexpressible holiness, God's awareness of people's dangerous and naive curiosity, and the life-threatening nature of God's presence in the people's present condition. Stuart observes that the warning may have been against those who out of curiosity to see God, see what was going on, or presume to get close to God would force their way up the mountain, thus reenacting the temptation in the garden of Eden. All of this communicates the awesome, life-threatening as well as life-giving nature of being in God's presence.[14] Consecration prepared them to be in God's presence, which entailed far more than physical proximity, though such proximity was an accessible way for the people to understand the reality.[15]

Belden Lane reflects, "There on the mountain, one meets the God of the unexpected. Yet Israel always held back from attributing a sense of automatic sacrality to mountain terrain. If a mountain was sacred, it was not because of its impressive height or any noumenal quality inherent in the place itself, but because Yahweh consented to be met there."[16] For Israel, being in the presence of the sovereign Creator of all and the Giver of all life brought them to the precipice of their mortality. They were to be poignantly aware of this reality in their relationship to God. To forget or ignore this would violate the relationship in the same way as had happened in the garden of Eden, and with similar consequence: death.

In Exodus 19:22 special emphasis is given to the fact that the priests had to consecrate themselves, otherwise "the Lord will break out against them." Having a special vocation to approach God did not

13. Gentry, "The Meaning of 'Holy,'" 407.

14. Gentry, "The Meaning of 'Holy,'" 431–32. See also Meyers, *Exodus*, 153.

15. This qualification is necessary in order not to raise unnecessary questions about God's omnipresence. For human beings to be in God's presence as portrayed in Exodus does not suggest that God was less than omnipresent. In consecration scenarios, God willed to be present, accessible, and knowable in a particular manner given the finite, fragile, and sinful human condition.

16. Lane, *Solace of Fierce Landscapes*, 45–46.

exempt priests from the need for consecration. They were no less fragile, finite, and sinful than the rest of the people. Childs insists that "the warning is given for the sake of the people, who have no experience as yet of the dimensions of divine holiness, and lest warned will destroy themselves."[17]

Yet, these ominous restrictions expressed God's merciful care for people as well as God's desire and provision for them to come as close as possible and still live. As John Oswalt rightly points out, in all of these stipulations God's purpose was "that they should be brought into relationship with him whereby he could live in their midst and his holiness would not destroy them."[18] God's intent to commune in a personal, protective, sustaining manner must never be obscured.

### *Exodus 28–29*

Several features stand out in this extended, descriptive command for the consecration of priests' garments and priests themselves. First is the repetition (e.g., 28:35, 43) that the purpose of consecration was that Aaron and his sons would not die in the Lord's presence. This reiterates God's desire and merciful provision for them actually to be in God's presence in their sinful, fragile state. Likewise, it reflects the people's need (vicariously expressed through the priests) to be in God's presence.

Second, the garments (interestingly, listed first in the descriptive order) to be consecrated were provisions external to the priests, given by the Lord to allow them into the divine presence and to protect them there. The parallel New Testament imagery of Christ's righteousness as a garment for the believer (e.g., Gal. 3:27; Eph. 4:24) is difficult to escape here.

Third, the purpose of these consecrated garments was also to allow the priests to receive guidance from God for the people and to bear the people's guilt before God in a representative manner. Meyers suggests that the priestly vestments "would symbolize the unseen presence

17. Childs, *Book of Exodus*, 370.

18. Oswalt, *Called to Be Holy*, 22. See also Toon, *Justification and Sanctification*, 37. There Toon underscores God's relational intent in the "act of making holy . . . [as] the transition from the realm of the profane to that of direct association with God."

of God and also would empower him to approach God and receive God's word. The tabernacle as a dwelling for God may have signified God's presence among the Israelites and secured divine availability. But in terms of communicating God's will to the people, the glorious sanctity of the priest arrayed in highly ceremonial garb was the key mechanism."[19] Although bearing guilt may be a function more familiar to many Christians, the function of receiving divine guidance indicates a purposeful, forward-looking trajectory for holiness. Consecration was necessary in order for God's people to navigate faithfully the complexities and challenges of life.

For the priests themselves, consecration involved being sprinkled with both anointing oil and sacrificial blood. Stuart explains, "In the logic of the Old Testament's revealed sacrificial system, oil helps signify purity and cleanness, but not forgiveness. The combination of the oil and the blood signify purity of service and forgiveness of sin respectively. Purity and forgiveness made the priests acceptable to God—'consecrated,' meaning 'holy.'"[20]

The remainder of Exodus 29 identifies three other objects of consecration: the sacrificial ram, the altar, and the tent of meeting. Counting the priests' garments, four nonhuman objects have now been designated for consecration, three of them inanimate. One of the two rams that were to be sacrificed was used to consecrate the priests' garments, and then (v. 27) parts of that ram were consecrated for the priests to eat. In both cases the consecrated part then belonged to the priests (vv. 27, 29, 33) for special use. Stuart underscores the significance of the grammatical construction used here: "This use of the *piel* of *qdš* reflects the sense of 'set aside for my use/the use that I specify.'"[21] Those divine purposes extend in 29:36–37 to the altar itself, which had to be atoned for and consecrated so that it would be holy and everything that touched it would be holy.

In Exodus 29:43 we see one of the most direct and definitive statements about how consecration occurs. The ritual acts were symbolic and instrumental, but the tent of meeting was consecrated directly

19. Meyers, *Exodus*, 244–45.
20. Stuart, *Exodus*, 625.
21. Stuart, *Exodus*, 627.

by God's glory. Stuart points out the significance of this: "In saying 'the place will be consecrated . . . by my glory,' God indicated the real means of sanctification—to which various sacrifices and rituals merely pointed—as his own presence. Where he is, he takes possession, and thus things near him become his and are holy."[22] A duplex sense of consecration thus appears. God consecrates by God's presence and, as seen in Exodus 19, consecration of people and objects was for preparation to be in God's presence and fulfill God's purposes. God's presence is key to consecration as both the active agency and the purpose. These acts of consecration culminated in verses 45–46 when God promised to dwell among the Israelites, reiterating from 6:6–7 the reminder of deliverance and the commitment to be their God.

### *Leviticus*

Leviticus records the enactment of God's consecration commands given in Exodus. Moses consecrated the tabernacle, all its utensils, Aaron and his sons, and their garments (chap. 8). God chose to dwell among these people, and God's covenantally defined, relational presence was localized to the tabernacle, thus establishing the consecration protocols for everyone and everything that came into God's presence.[23]

Leviticus 11 highlights again the consecration of the entire people of Israel, recorded in Exodus 19, for the special occasion of approaching Mount Sinai to meet with God. In Leviticus 11 and 20, however, God called the people to be consecrated or holy in their entire way of being because that was who they were in covenantal relationship to God. They were to be holy because God had delivered them from Egypt, because God had made personal commitment to them, and because God is holy. These divine claims formed the basis for their new identity, which was to be lived out distinctively in all that they did.

Fleming Rutledge draws attention to how God's holiness-based, holiness-oriented purposes for Israel boldly contrasted to all that surrounded them:

22. Stuart, *Exodus*, 631.

23. Levering, *Doctrine of the Holy Spirit*, 345–46. Levering highlights the connection that Thomas Aquinas drew between holiness and the indwelling presence of God.

> Most of the actual ordinances in Leviticus are inconceivable to us today, but with a little extra effort we can grasp the significance of the "holiness" to which God's people are called. . . . The purpose of living "apart" is to glorify Israel's God in the midst of a rampaging pagan culture. The only way this can be done is by a distinct way of life. God's people adhere to a different mode of existence in the world, one that proclaims the true God over against the "gods many and lords many" that Paul spoke of to the Corinthian church.[24]

Leviticus 20:7–8 brings together the divine and human acts of consecration: "Consecrate yourselves therefore, and be holy" and "I sanctify you." These are bracketed by stern ethical imperatives on either side and held together by twin divine assertions: "I am the LORD your God" and "I am the LORD." Here we see a pattern that will be followed throughout the canon of Scripture. God claims people, commits to those people, sets them apart, and with undiluted force commands them to live out the implications of what God has done to consecrate them.[25]

Identity, mission, and ethical imperatives converge in Leviticus in mutually defining and enriching ways, preventing identity from becoming ingrown and self-serving, mission from becoming programmatic and one-dimensional, and ethical imperatives from becoming moralistic and external. For Israel, consecration intrinsically brought them back to God's personal commitment to them, presence with them, and purposes for them, which were constantly to shape them ethically. These themes resurface later in Israel's history under Joshua's leadership.

#### *Joshua*

Two vignettes in the book of Joshua reinforce the life-altering effects of consecration. In Joshua 3 Israel was about to cross the Jordan River, another occasion for the display of God's power and commitment to this nation. To prepare for what was certainly a terrifying

24. Rutledge, *Crucifixion*, 242.

25. My Old Testament colleague Knut Heim suggests that this may be the most significant consecration passage in the entire Hebrew canon because of all the consecration features present in it.

prospect to many Israelites, despite what God had already done in leading a previous generation across the Red Sea, Joshua instructed the people to consecrate themselves. This act of consecration likely involved a renewed commitment of faith and was specifically focused on Joshua's assurance that "tomorrow the LORD will do wonders among you" (v. 5). Trent Butler treats this as another instance of God drawing uniquely near for another act of deliverance: "Israel is to sanctify herself, literally 'make yourselves holy.' This involved a purification ritual which prepares a person to enter the divine presence."[26]

The second instance of consecration is recorded in Joshua 7 and had an equally auspicious, though somewhat different, character. Israel had gone to battle against Ai and been roundly defeated. When Joshua passionately inquired why God had led them to that place and allowed their defeat, God exposed the sin (though not the sinner). When they had defeated Jericho, God had specifically instructed them not to take the "devoted things" from the city. Yet one man, Achan, had done so (indicating the communal implications of individual acts). God would not be with them, Joshua was told, "unless you destroy the devoted things from among you" (v. 12). God's presence—or lack of presence—with them was again the central and defining issue.

Prior to Achan's exposure God told Joshua to consecrate the people (v. 13). That consecration was in preparation for a chilling purge of Israel's sin, which, though committed by one individual, was counted as the sin of the people. Once they were cleansed of this sin, God would be present with them yet again and lead them to victory. Butler comments, "The key promise to Joshua in the book is the presence of God (1:5, 9; 3:7). Divine presence is the prayer of the people for Joshua (1:17), the basis of Joshua's exaltation (3:7) and the hope of possessing the land (3:10). Passing over the covenant has let all this pass away. . . . Obedient people will destroy the banned goods in their midst and again experience divine presence. Israel must choose between the presence of God (v 12) and the presence of חרם [*haram*] (v 13)."[27]

With consecration framing the incident, Butler's observations point again to the character and purpose of consecration. Richard

26. Butler, *Joshua*, 46.
27. Butler, *Joshua*, 85.

Nelson reinforces the point, pulling into view previous accounts of consecration: "Sanctification is commanded (v. 13) to prepare for firsthand contact with Yahweh's activity (3:5; Exod. 19:10–11) and perhaps also to counter the effects of contagious *herem*."[28] God's presence is not static but active. To be in God's presence is to encounter God's power in one form or another. God is not only the giver and taker of life but also the changer of life.

### *1 Kings*

First Kings 9 offers an account of consecration in which God's presence is associated with God's name. In this case, God consecrated Solomon's temple by placing the divine name there. This blessing was followed by the threefold warning that if Israel was disobedient, they would be cut off from the promised land. If this warning was actualized, God's presence would be withdrawn through God's rejection of the temple that God had consecrated by and for God's name.

Peter Leithart elaborates on the significant connection between God's presence and God's name:

> At the temple dedication, Solomon requested that the Lord hear prayers at the temple, and in this second dream Yahweh promises to keep his eyes open in the house perpetually. The Lord's answer shows that Yahweh's relationship to the temple is not "distant" or "reserved." Yahweh promises to put his "name" at the temple . . . as well as his "eyes" and "heart." By these, Yahweh "consecrates" (הקדשתי) the house, which shows that Yahweh is present in the temple, since sanctuaries are consecrated by his advent in glory (Exod. 29:43).[29]

The notion that the divine name has power may seem strange to many in post-Enlightenment, Western culture for whom the descriptive, locutionary character of language is more familiar and for whom names have a largely denotative function. Stanley Grenz points out, however, that the giving of God's name was the giving of God's self, particularly in faithful relationship.[30] Here again on

28. Nelson, *Joshua*, 105.
29. Leithart, *1 & 2 Kings*, 71.
30. Grenz, *The Named God*, 150–51.

display are the striking, breathtaking implications of God's presence for the act of consecration. The presence of God is inherently relational.

### *1 Chronicles*

The ark of the covenant represented or localized God's presence, perhaps more poignantly than any other entity or place. The role of the ark with God's people (e.g., Josh. 3–7; 1 Sam. 4:21–22) makes this clear. First Chronicles 15:12 records, "He [David] said to them, 'You are the heads of families of the Levites; sanctify yourselves, you and your kindred, so that you may bring up the ark of the LORD, the God of Israel, to the place that I have prepared for it.'" In light of the divine presence, the strict responsibilities involved with transporting the ark convey the auspicious character of that act and the consequences of careless missteps (2 Sam. 6:6–7). Thus, consecration was essential for those who would tend to the ark because they would be working directly with that which God had chosen to mediate God's presence.

### *2 Chronicles*

The austere implications of consecration emerge again in 2 Chronicles 7:19–20 with God's consecration of the temple with God's name: "But if you turn aside and forsake my statutes and my commandments that I have set before you, and go and serve others gods and worship them, then I will pluck you up from the land that I have given you; and this house, which I have consecrated for my name, I will cast out of my sight, and will make it a proverb and a byword among all peoples." Consecration of the temple was for the sake of relating to God's presence and relationship to God's people. Disobedience to God would result in the loss of that special relationship that the temple provided.

### *Zephaniah 1:7*

Be silent before the Lord GOD! For the day of the LORD is at hand; the LORD has prepared a sacrifice, he has consecrated his guests.

O. Palmer Robertson notes, "In this context of the presentation of the Day of Yahweh in connection with covenant inauguration and enforcement, Zephaniah declares that *Yahweh has prepared a sacrifice* and *sanctified his guests* (Zeph. 1:7). Both of these actions are closely associated with the establishment of the covenant in the traditions of Israel."[31] Zephaniah's prophecy underscores the covenantal purposes and the presence of God involved in consecration.

## Conclusion

With our theology of sanctification adequately rooted in the Old Testament practice of consecration, we can see God's presence and purposes as the definitive orientation. Hans Urs von Balthasar points out how the unique character of God's love both liberated and called the people of Israel for their unique role in the world: "For all those who personally remain close to the presence of God are as individuals accounted 'holy' (see Ps. 17:3; 34:10, 18)."[32] Consecration was a dynamic and relational reality.

Consecration signified God's gracious work of taking ownership of God's people, then commissioning the people to extend that blessing beyond themselves. Ivor Davidson makes this point:

> If we would learn what holiness is, it is to covenantal history that we are directed. . . . It is as he establishes fellowship with these naturally unholy ones that he is seen for who he is. He summons unlikely people, sets them apart, purifies them, makes them his treasured possession. The ethical entailments of that appointment are substantial and public-facing: they are to testify before the nations as to his character (Ex 19:5–6). "Be holy, for I am holy," Israel is commanded (Lev 11:44; 19:2; cf. 20:7); their conduct is to declare it. . . . He calls them to show they belong to him and none other. Yet even there the obligation is framed in a context of grace, for he is himself the primary agent of their sanctification—"the Lord, who makes you holy" (Lev 20:8 NIV; see also Lev 21:8).[33]

31. Robertson, *Nahum, Habakkuk, and Zephaniah*, 269 (emphasis original).
32. Balthasar, *Engagement with God*, 21.
33. Davidson, "Gospel Holiness," 197.

The larger context of consecration was covenantal relationship with God, the demand for faithfulness to the unique identity and purposes given in that covenantal relationship, and preparation for being in proximity to God's presence. Considered apart from this context, the familiar and often-emphasized cleansing aspect easily becomes self-referential and diverts attention from the larger issues in consecration. The Old Testament vignettes we have examined bring the context and purposes of consecration back into vivid focus. Covenant, missional purpose, and God's presence anchor and animate the practice of consecration so that the instrumental aspects, such as cleansing, do not become isolated or out of proportion and thus either lifeless or distorted.

Anytime a person or an object (we will examine more about the inanimate realm in chap. 5) was consecrated, people knew or should have known that serious business with God was about to take place. The primary focal point of the act, however, was not the person or object to be consecrated. The focus was God, God's presence, God's covenantal commitment and call, and God's faithfulness. These were the operative factors—the dynamic realities that then compelled and changed people.

In light of these features, consecration had unavoidable implications for the way people lived and, by further implication, the type of people they were habitually to become. In the New Testament we find this expressed in ethical imperatives and sometimes called "transformation." However, the biblical profile that has emerged thus far raises questions about whether the dominant, controlling emphases discerned in holiness have shifted over time toward the ethical and transformational. What would be different in our understanding and pursuit of holiness if those proportions were realigned with the pattern of emphasis we have observed? As the New Testament picks up the concept of consecration with terminology often translated as "sanctification," the same themes and patterns will resurface, yet with even more stunning implications.

# 4

# A Shocking New Story

## *Sanctification in the New Testament*

The doctrine of sanctification that weaves throughout much of the New Testament builds directly on the Old Testament's presentation of consecration. It extended those Old Testament threads into the lives of all who belong to God through Jesus Christ, Jews and gentiles alike, altering how they understood themselves, how they responded to God, and how they engaged both other believers and the world around them. It was an impactful new story for them.

As with the Old Testament, this survey of New Testament texts will be representative rather than exhaustive, and will seek to clarify what actually is and is not said in each case. In the process it will become evident that certain assumptions have accrued in various renditions of sanctification, some of which are neither biblically conclusive nor uniformly constructive for Christian living.

As the New Testament evidence is scrutinized, two traits become evident. By far the quantity of evidence for sanctification resides in the accomplished category, with various subdivisions of emphasis. Of greater significance, however, is that this evidence for accomplished sanctification suggests that it functions as a controlling framework for texts that speak of sanctification in imperatival terms or as yet to be fulfilled.

The widespread pattern of focusing primarily on sanctification imperatives and promises tends to portray sanctification as synonymous with transformation and gives minimal attention to the accomplished aspect of sanctification. This tendency leads into precarious territory theologically, experientially, and pastorally. Imperatives and eschatological allusions to sanctification must be interpreted, just as they are given, in light of the accomplished sanctification that undergirds and defines them.

## Sanctified Introductions

The most frequently overlooked sanctification texts are the introductory remarks in numerous epistles. In modern correspondence, introductions are often treated as throwaway lines, quickly glossed over and ignored in order to get to what we assume is the heart of the correspondence. "Dear _____. How are you? Hope you are well. What's new? Blah, blah, blah. . . . (Now, here's what I really want to say!)." We are impoverished when we read the introductory remarks of biblical correspondence in this manner. Apostolic greetings are thick and poignant with theological implications about sanctification. These introductory words should grab our attention because they continue the trajectory set by the Old Testament texts and drive down theological pylons for the more explicit sanctification texts. To glide past these statements allows the sanctification imperatives to take on layers of meaning that do not naturally belong to them.

David Powlison points out, "In the Bible itself, the word *sanctify* is most often used in the past tense. It describes something that has already happened. It is one of describing how God decisively acts to make you his own."[1] This should make us question why so little is made of this fact and how it is significant, especially for the imperatival and future dimensions of sanctification. The following introductory greetings reflect the basic and defining view that the apostolic writers held of their readers.

1. Powlison, *How Does Sanctification Work?*, 113n1.

- **Romans 1:7:** "To all God's beloved in Rome, who are called to be saints"
- **1 Corinthians 1:2a:** "To the church of God that is in Corinth, to those who are sanctified in Christ Jesus, called to be saints"
- **2 Corinthians 1:1b:** "To the church of God that is in Corinth, including all the saints throughout Achaia"
- **Ephesians 1:1b:** "To the saints who are in Ephesus and are faithful in Christ Jesus"
- **Philippians 1:1b:** "To all the saints in Christ Jesus who are in Philippi, with the bishops and deacons"
- **Colossians 1:2a:** "To the saints and faithful brothers and sisters in Christ in Colossae"
- **1 Peter 1:1b–2:** "To the exiles of the Dispersion in Pontus, Galatia, Cappadocia, Asia, and Bithynia, who have been chosen and destined by God the Father and sanctified by the Spirit to be obedient to Jesus Christ and to be sprinkled with his blood"

At least three features stand out from these introductions. First, some of the introductions include the dual sense that the Christians addressed were holy already and that they were called to be holy. Past, present, and future come together. Second, the themes of God's calling, choosing, and electing are linked to God's work of sanctification. Third, sanctification is defined by being "in Christ Jesus." Even when the term "positional" is used theologically to describe what is said in texts such as these, "in Christ" provides a relational point of reference that transcends any sort of spatial or even formal theological position. The role of the Holy Spirit appears in that same relational sense.

Not least in significance, Paul's Corinthian correspondence particularly reflects the fact that sanctification characterized Christians who were quite immature and, to state it bluntly, an ethical mess! That makes it easy to see accomplished sanctification as something God has already and decisively done, which on a practical level reinforces God's expectations for them. Yet, how might God's expectations (e.g., the imperatives) function differently if they were read in light of the force of what had already been accomplished?

It should be noted that behind most forms of "saint," "holy," and "sanctify" lay some form of the word *hagios* (ἅγιος). *Hagios* is used in Luke 2:23 to translate *qādôš* (קדשׁ) when Luke quotes Exodus 13:2, providing an example of the link between consecration in the Old Testament and sanctification in the New Testament. C. E. B. Cranfield comments on the use of *hagioi* in Romans 1:7:

> The term ἅγιος also has a significant history. The root meaning of *ḳāḏôš* seems to be "marked off," "separate," "withdrawn from ordinary use." Whereas in the paganism surrounding Israel it was applied predominantly to objects, places and human persons, and only rarely to the actual deity, in the OT it is chiefly of God Himself that it is used, and the holiness of places, objects and human persons is hardly ever conceived in a merely impersonal, mechanical sense, but is thought of as derived from the personal will of God and therefore always involving an encounter with the personal demands of the living God who claims the absolute allegiance of His people. It is this difference, and not simply its ethical content, as is sometimes alleged, which distinguishes the OT conception of holiness from the pagan. . . . The term "holy," applied to Israel, expressed the fact that they were God's special people. Their holiness derived from God's gracious choice, and it involved the obligation on their part to seek to be and do what was in accordance with the revealed character of their God by obedience to His law. . . . Paul's use of ἅγιος rests squarely upon this OT foundation.[2]

Regarding Paul's introduction to the Corinthians, Roy Ciampa and Brian Rosner observe the following:

> The church in Corinth consists of *those sanctified in Christ Jesus*. . . . *Sanctified* here is a perfect passive participle, which, according to recent studies of verbal aspect, stresses the present state of affairs. Thanks to Christ's work on the cross, believers find themselves in a state of sanctification (are now sanctified), made acceptable to God (Rom. 15:16) and able to enter into and enjoy his presence. . . . Sanctification in the New Testament generally does not refer primarily to growth in holiness but to God's taking possession of believers.[3]

2. Cranfield, *Epistle to the Romans*, 1:70.
3. Ciampa and Rosner, *First Letter to the Corinthians*, 55–56 (emphasis original).

References to sanctification such as these introductory comments reinforce the theological significance of accomplished sanctification because they establish connections with other key biblical themes such as election, belonging, and living in God's presence. Accomplished sanctification has a deeply relational character.

Anthony Thiselton drives this point home by noting, "The readers' status as those who belong to God and are called to live out this godly holiness *derives from their being-in-Christ*."[4] The full impact of those connections is yet to be seen, but even at this point it should not be lost on us that proximity to God's presence and intimacy with God, available only selectively and in a mediated sense in the Old Testament, are now available to all who are in Christ by the Holy Spirit. One can only imagine how staggering this prospect would have been to the Israelites—that potentially anyone would have access to God in the same manner as the priests did in their day! Apparently, Paul and Peter intended this reality to have the same arresting and compelling impact on all followers of Jesus after the breathtaking outpouring of the Spirit at Pentecost.

These introductory apostolic remarks, along with other New Testament references to sanctification as accomplished, bolster and thicken the indicative aspect of the well-known "indicative–imperative" formulation. When "indicative" is understood merely as a descriptive category, it fails to capture fully or vibrantly that which has already decisively been done by God to sanctify us through Jesus Christ.

Regardless of the wording used, the scant amount of attention to biblical texts that clearly declare sanctification as an accomplished reality is curious and troubling, even though this oversight has been challenged previously.[5] Fleming Rutledge helpfully clarifies the indicative–imperative relationship when commenting on Romans 12:1–2:

4. Thiselton, *First Epistle to the Corinthians*, 76 (emphasis original).

5. David Peterson poured an important base layer to this foundation in *Possessed by God*, pointing out that many familiar New Testament texts commonly understood to connote progressive growth actually refer to accomplished (what he refers to as "positional") sanctification. His work has been frequently cited and sometimes critiqued (as in Allen, *Sanctification*), but his basic point is difficult either to ignore or to refute. For further exegetical support of Peterson's work, see J. Howard, *Paul, the Community, and Progressive Sanctification*.

"The imperative is not only *dependent upon* but *organically produced by* the indicative, or declarative, proclamation."[6] She draws attention to the fact that sanctification functions as a verbal noun—a noun that inherently involves action. God's act of sanctifying people through the work of Jesus Christ is not merely a first and formal condition for transformation. God's act decisively creates a transforming relational reality "in Christ."

Recalibration of the doctrine of sanctification through resuscitation of accomplished sanctification requires fresh attention to the triune agency at work in sanctification—that is, the role of the Son and the Spirit.[7] Peter Toon identifies the christologically focused work of the Spirit as the crucial difference between Old and New Testaments. The Spirit's work also suggests continuity between consecration and sanctification, since "the Holy Spirit as the Paraclete *sets people apart* for God in the name of Jesus, the Holy One and Messiah. They can be *set apart* for God because of the sacrificial blood of Jesus, shed for the remission of their sins (Heb. 10:29). We are *set apart* for God by the atoning work of Christ, and we are *set apart* for God in the work of the Holy Spirit."[8] Although the Holy Spirit's role in sanctification is rarely contested, overlooking the Spirit's role in accomplished sanctification malnourishes every other aspect of sanctification.

## Sanctification as Accomplished

At this point our attention turns to texts that more directly and deeply elucidate the powerful nature of accomplished sanctification. Exhaustive exposition of these texts would go far beyond the scope of the study, but a few observations will suffice to demonstrate the pattern.

### *1 Corinthians 6:11*

> And this [sexually immoral, idolaters, etc., in vv. 9–10] is what some of you used to be. But you were washed, you were sanctified, you

6. Rutledge, *Crucifixion*, 558 (emphasis original).

7. T. A. Noble's incisive work in *Holy Trinity: Holy People* provides essential trinitarian nutrients for the doctrine of sanctification.

8. Toon, *Justification and Sanctification*, 39 (emphasis added).

were justified in the name of the Lord Jesus Christ and in the Spirit of our God.

Gordon Fee calls this "one of the most important theological statements in the epistle."[9] Recall the significance of the fact that Paul wrote these words to a church that, in his estimation, was horribly immature and in many ways not living out the implications of the gospel. "Washed" (*apelousasthe*, ἀπελούσασθε) depicts their experience of forgiveness and their entry into salvation. Likewise, "justified" or "made righteous" (*edikaiōthēte*, ἐδικαιώθητε) continues to receive robust scholarly attention. However, "sanctified" (*hēgiasthēte*, ἡγιάσθητε) finds itself eclipsed by the concepts on either side. Yet, as Fee contends, "since the three verbs refer to the same reality, and since each of them has 'God' as the implied subject, the two prepositional phrases are to be understood as modifying all three verbs."[10]

In the immediately preceding context Paul rebukes them for taking one another to court and equates that practice with spiritual defeat (v. 7) and wrongdoing. He goes on to list other types of wrongdoing that are incompatible with the kingdom of God (vv. 9–10). Then he strenuously affirms their new identity, contrasting it not only with their former practices but also with the former identity that generated those practices. In other words, to Paul, that is not who they currently were! Their new identity was not merely a new status but a new relationship defined by God's *acts* on their behalf through Jesus and by the Spirit. That is, in Christ they *already were* new people, even though severely lacking in behavioral conformity to that newness.

Their sanctification (along with their cleansing and justification) constituted this new reality and the basis for his appeal to a different way of living. Paul's moral imperatives emerged from the reality of who God had made them to be and the fact that God actively dwelt among them. They were in fact different people, not in the sense of having a new formal status or God simply "seeing" them differently but because of God's active presence and agency in their lives.

9. Fee, *First Epistle to the Corinthians*, 245.
10. Fee, *First Epistle to the Corinthians*, 246.

Matthew Levering draws on Psalm 93 to make this very point: "God dwells in his people as a sanctifying power, not as a passive inhabitant. Furthermore, the indwelling of the Trinity is not simply an individual experience but rather is the fulfillment of God's covenantal promises to his people."[11] Something decisive and powerful had happened to them, as indicated by the way Paul set up this contrast.

Paul extends his argument in the balance of the chapter when he appeals for them to avoid sexual immorality based on the Holy Spirit's indwelling presence in their lives. Thus, what they did with their bodies had profound moral implications. Sexual immorality was unthinkable and utterly incongruous with the presence of the Living God in their lives through the Spirit. God's presence in them and among them signified that they belonged to God and not to themselves.

This is part of what happens when someone or something is sanctified. God takes ownership (and occupancy)[12] by the Spirit for God's purposes. The body is no longer common or to be used in any way one pleases. Sanctification involves a new identity because of new ownership, new indwelling, and new purposes. To act in conflict with this accomplished sanctification is far more than to contradict a formal fact. It reflects the relentless tendency to forget God's decisive acts and thus to squelch and work against the life-giving and life-transforming presence of God.

English translations do not always show how in the Greek text the adversative "but" (*alla*, ἀλλά) precedes each key verb, which intensifies Paul's point. Fee argues that this "gives additional force to the 'once you were, but now you are not' emphasis of the sentence."[13] Furthermore, through the sanctifying aspect of this trifold saving work, "God . . . has already begun the work of ethical transformation."[14] Fee suggests that the two prepositional phrases, "in the name of the Lord Jesus Christ" and "in the Spirit of our God," though using the same Greek construction (*en*, ἐν), most likely function instrumentally (i.e., they can be translated as "by the Lord Jesus Christ" and "by the

11. Levering, *Doctrine of the Holy Spirit*, 346.
12. Note again the title of Peterson's work: *Possessed by God*.
13. Fee, *First Epistle to the Corinthians*, 246.
14. Fee, *First Epistle to the Corinthians*, 248.

Spirit of our God").[15] That is, through the Spirit's work in all three divine acts, the realities of the future are already powerfully at work in the present age.

"The Corinthian problem," Fee claims, "was not with their experience of the Spirit, but with their misunderstanding of what it meant to be Spirit people."[16] The indicative behind the imperative is dynamically and relationally charged by its roots in the triune agency. Though sanctification and transformation are not presented as synonymous, they are powerfully linked. God's active, sanctifying presence works to change us. Sanctification is inconceivable apart from the Holy Spirit because the Spirit represents the presence of the Living God. Stated more positively, the Spirit is the objective reality of sanctification, and where the Spirit is, there is sanctification. Where there is sanctification, there is—there must be—transformation.

It is important to reiterate here that the adjective "accomplished," when used to describe the Spirit's sanctifying work as seen in 1 Corinthians 6:11, does not refer to a level of spiritual maturity or moral character. The accomplished nature of sanctification signals an entirely new relationship with God in and through the presence and work of God the Holy Spirit and in union with Jesus Christ. Moral and ethical transformation are motivated, resourced, and set in motion by this sanctification. In Paul's mind, transformation had already begun and must continue due to accomplished sanctification.

### *Hebrews 10:10*

> And it is by God's will that we have been sanctified through the offering of the body of Jesus Christ once for all.

15. Fee, *First Epistle to the Corinthians*, 247.

16. Fee, *First Epistle to the Corinthians*, 248. In "We Are the Circumcision," Lynn Cohick shows that in the Philippian correspondence Paul was addressing an undercurrent of controversy about how holiness relates to circumcision. The key question addressed by the Jerusalem Council had been "What is holiness?" and that same question disrupted the church at Philippi. Cohick demonstrates how Paul drew on the conclusion of the Jerusalem Council to convince the Philippians that the Holy Spirit constitutes the definitive identity of believers, and thus the presence of the Spirit is the basis of holiness. This corroborates the explicit theological point made in Acts 15:8–9. The power of accomplished sanctification was demonstrated by the fact that God had cleansed and given the Spirit to the gentiles.

The book of Hebrews presents perhaps the most widely acknowledged affirmations of sanctification as an accomplished reality. This statement succinctly captures a vital result of Christ's sacrificial death on our behalf, the sufficiency of which the writer has argued up to this point in the epistle. F. F. Bruce remarks, "The sanctification which His people receive in consequence is their inward cleansing from sin and their being made fit for the presence of God, so that henceforth they can offer Him acceptable worship. It is a sanctification that has taken place once for all."[17] "Fit for the presence of God" and the capacity for worship portray something of the dynamic character of this sanctification.

The notions of cleansing and being in God's presence are not unfamiliar to those acquainted with Hebrews and its theology. Yet, the Old Testament backdrop of consecration suggests a gravitas—a sobering but grateful tenor—to this affirmation of God's auspicious, accompanying presence. What God has done is incredible. Equally stunning is the fact that this is made so widely accessible to ordinary people. The writer of this epistle was concerned either that the recipients had not fully grasped this reality or that it had become benign to them, in either case leaving them unresponsive to God and vulnerable to the allure of retreat to Judaism when under the duress of persecution from the Roman Empire.

Gareth Cockerill highlights the interactive, responsive implications of this sanctifying act: "One cannot reduce this holiness to a legal standing, nor can one identify it with perfection of life. Christ has set his people apart for God by cleansing them from the pollution and dominion of sin (9:14) so that they can enter the divine presence where they receive the 'mercy' of continual cleansing and the 'grace' for perseverance in obedience (4:16)."[18] This sanctifying act, then, turns out to contain vast and potent resources for the life of faith, not simply because of a formal status before God or a personal state (of spirituality or maturity) in the human believer but because the sanctifying act provides entrance to the very presence of God, from whence the resources for faithfulness and perseverance in trial come. Faithful living depends on accomplished sanctification.

17. Bruce, *Epistle to the Hebrews*, 236.
18. Cockerill, *Epistle to the Hebrews*, 443.

***Hebrews 10:29***

How much worse punishment do you think will be deserved by those who have spurned the Son of God, profaned the blood of the covenant by which they were sanctified, and outraged the Spirit of grace?

Apart from the theologically controversial issues raised by this text, the sobering character of God's sanctifying act stands out clearly. God's covenant represents God's personal investment. God's very self is present to the covenant in love and veracity. Flaunting that divine love and the response that it commands through willful and continued sin (10:26)—to trample underfoot the Son of God (cf. 10:29 ESV)—equates to thumbing one's nose at God.

To "outrage the Spirit of grace" is to rebuff, despise, and dismiss the person of God through the Spirit, inasmuch as grace is always personal and not an impersonal, discrete substance.[19] These features of this warning highlight the weightiness of accomplished sanctification. To live with such disregard for one's sanctification is to disregard the very presence of God. If we focus on these warnings in isolation, we can easily miss their linkage to the personal and covenantal character of God's sanctifying act.

Admittedly, theological questions remain about the nature of the spiritual risk presented, the eternal standing of the person(s) in view, and what it means for such a person to have been sanctified. These important issues aside, the severity of the risk in "trampling" and "outraging" is magnified in light of what sanctification represents. The writer intends the stark contrast to have a biting effect and leave the reader with a deep, visceral sense of awe and motivation. Accomplished sanctification has power—the power of God—in our lives.

19. The assumption that grace is a discrete substance ("its own thing"), which originates with God but is detachable from the person and presence of God, gained currency in late medieval Roman Catholic theology via the framework of Aristotelian metaphysics. Grace became understood as a substance that all people need for salvation, allotted first to the church, and then dispensed by the church through various sacraments. The lingering and ripple effects of this paradigm on Protestants has been incalculable, even apart from the concept's ecclesiological and sacramental packaging in Roman Catholic theology.

#### *1 Peter 1:22*

Now that you have purified your souls by your obedience to the truth so that you have a genuine mutual love, love one another deeply from the heart.

Peter bases this call to love on his addresses' prior (both logically and chronologically) act of purification (*hēgnikotes*, ἡγνικότες). John Elliott draws attention to connections established in this text between the Old Testament, the broader concept of holiness, and union with Christ: "The verb *hagnizō*, 'purify,' in the LXX and NT often denotes ceremonial purification of objects . . . or people. . . . But here . . . it denotes moral purification, as the reference to 'obedience' makes clear. . . . Thus, the verb functions as a synonym of 'being holy' . . . stressing union with God and separation from former impurity."[20] Peter's linkage of purification, obedience to the truth, and love prevents purification from being understood in an individualistic, pietistic manner. This triad of purification, obedience, and love has even richer implications, as indicated by the reference point of obedience—the truth.

Karen Jobes translates *hēgnikotes* as "consecrated" and highlights the present perfect tense of the verb, "indicating that they are now in the state of having been set apart by their previous obedience to the gospel."[21] Identifying obedience to the truth as the instrumental factor in purification/consecration, Peter likely is recalling Jesus's words recorded in John 17:17, 19: "Sanctify them in the truth; your word is truth. . . . And for their sakes I sanctify myself, so that they also may be sanctified in truth."

Jesus had identified himself as "the truth" (John 14:6), declared the disciples "clean" (though with a different word: *katharoi*, καθαροί [13:10]) because of what he had taught them (15:3), instructed them to abide in him (15:4), commanded them to love one another (15:12), linked himself with the "word" (17:17; just as John had done in 1:1, 14), and equated "word" and "truth" (17:17). It is reasonable

20. Elliott, *1 Peter*, 382–83. The same point is made by Davids, *First Epistle of Peter*, 76.

21. Jobes, *1 Peter*, 123.

to assume that Peter drew on that set of connections to shape his expectations for and exhortations to these believers.

The "truth" they had obeyed was Jesus—the Word. The "Word" (*logos*, λόγος) designates both the incarnate Son and the message or gospel of Christ (e.g., Acts 6:7; 11:1). Obedience to the truth is obedience to the gospel, which is obedience to Jesus Christ. Through this obedience they had sanctified themselves to God just as Jesus had, and had placed themselves in the realm of God's love, where Jesus had prayed they would be (John 17:26). (The significance of Jesus's sanctification will be further developed in chapter 5.)

Jobes underscores this point: "The Christian's decision to obey the truth by coming to faith in Christ is the manifestation of one's rebirth as a child of God (1:3). Peter instructs that love between Christians involves a moral transformation following from the spiritual reality that those reborn from God's seed will have God's character."[22] The obedience to which Peter cryptically refers implies the potent work of God underneath or inside their act of purification.

Taken together with the other Johannine themes that Peter appears also to have had in mind, this purification is inseparable from participation in and expression of the love of God, into which they had been drawn by their faith-based abiding in Jesus Christ. In this one brief statement, Peter acknowledges that the believers he addresses shared in the same relational intimacy with God that was given to him as an apostle by the Lord himself in those early days—all as a result of sanctification.

## Conclusion

Sanctification forms the basis and framework for obedient conformity to the image of Christ. Sanctification must be responded to and lived out, and must permeate all aspects of our lives, thus leading to maturity. According to Paul, faith, the subjective indicator of sanctification, marks our identity and opens God's resurrection power

22. Jobes, *1 Peter*, 125. See also Schreiner, *1, 2 Peter, Jude*, 92–93.

(the power of the Spirit [Rom. 8:11]) to us. In that way we may know Christ and in that knowing become like Christ.

Accomplished sanctification does not refer to the completion of our character, a level of spiritual maturity, or any particular experiential state in our relationship with God. Nor does it eliminate effort and responsibility to grow. Rather, this biblically dominating aspect of sanctification is framed by God's covenant promise and faithfulness and is brought about by the Holy Spirit. In accomplished sanctification we are cleansed from sin, set apart for God's purposes, and situated constantly in the presence of the Living God.

These realities begin to illuminate the link between sanctification and transformation—specifically, how sanctification leads to transformation. Through sanctification we have been fitted to live in the presence of God and empowered to respond to this God who, as holy love, self-reveals to us and redeems us through the person and gospel of Jesus Christ. Attending, submitting, and orienting our lives to God thus revealed cannot help but change us. We can attend, submit, and orient our lives in genuinely transformative ways only because of what has taken place in sanctification.

Sanctification presents us with everything we need to pursue and live out the implications of holiness—including our responsibility to do so. Holiness has a specific shape. It is not anything that any, perhaps well-intentioned or pious, religious tradition wants to make it. The shape and the character of holiness are found in Jesus Christ. Thus, sanctification provides the template for our transformation.

John Webster highlights how sanctification's gospel-dependent character, especially in ecclesial context, mitigates the risks of moralism that impede the healthy pursuit and realization of transformation:

> How, then, is the Church holy? By attention and submission to the gospel as the indicative of election and the imperative of obedience. . . . The Church is consecrated by the Father's resolve, holy in Christ and sanctified by the Holy Spirit. Such holiness is not achieved perfection, but an alien holiness which is the contradiction of its very real sinfulness. . . . This means that, far from being a matter of confident purity, holiness is visible as humble acknowledgement of sin and as prayer for forgiveness. . . .

> In effect, the rooting of sanctification in justification prohibits any conversion of sanctification into ethical self-improvement, as if justification were merely an initial infusion of capacities which are then activated through moral or spiritual exertion. Moreover, tying sanctification so firmly to divine agency enters a protest against exemplarist accounts of the atonement in which the work of Christ is reduced to the mere occasion, stimulus or pattern for the Christian's efforts to become holy through works of holiness.[23]

Sanctification is far more than, and far more robust than, a repackaged version of moral improvement, a weight that makes followers of Jesus sag and sigh when reminded of it. It is more than deepened spiritual impulses, inclinations, and sensibilities. It is integral to God's overall work of redemption. Sanctification should sober us, but just as much, bring us joy and hope. It should inflame our hunger to pursue and respond to God, stunned perhaps by the inconceivable reality that we have been chosen for, fitted for, and drawn into the very presence of God in the same sense that the high priest experienced (only once a year!) under the old covenant. We can and must be transformed because we have been sanctified.

Sanctification must never be seen as an end in itself, lest its extrinsic focus be lost. Nor must transformation ever be detached from sanctification, lest moralism overrun us by isolating the imperatival and futuristic aspects from their moorings. Before turning to those texts, however, we must examine some unexpected and easily overlooked instances of sanctification in the New Testament. These turn out to reinforce the biblical profile that has been emerging.

23. Webster, *Holiness*, 73, 81.

# 5

# Unexpected Instances of Sanctification

The impact of the doctrine of sanctification on believers' lives depends largely on how these three strands—accomplished, imperatival, and yet to be completed—relate to one another. Are they simply three equal and parallel emphases? Or does one of them shine the light in which the others are to be seen? This question of proportion and function makes enormous difference in how believers respond to each strand. The composite profile that emerges from representative texts makes the most sense if the accomplished nature of sanctification is understood as the defining and illuminating theme.

The case for the dominance of accomplished sanctification in the biblical profile is bolstered by emphases found in three rather unusual or unexpected examples of sanctification. These instances are Jesus's own sanctification, the sanctification of unbelieving spouses and unbelieving children of believers, and the sanctification of inanimate objects. Each of these displays the motifs that have anchored the doctrine of sanctification all along, even with their controversial nature and lingering exegetical questions.

## Jesus's Sanctification

The dominant character of accomplished sanctification receives additional, though overlooked, support from Jesus's reference to his own sanctification. This part of the study rounds out the profile by considering the One not only in whom we are sanctified but who himself is the Sanctified One. How have so many approaches to sanctification seemingly not allowed themselves to be shaped directly by Jesus's own sanctification? This neglect has contributed to disproportionate emphases and overassociation of sanctification with transformation. Yet, Jesus spoke of his own sanctification in ways that should set the pace for how all who follow him understand their sanctification.

Jesus's prayer for the disciples' sanctification was underwritten by his own sanctification. His sanctification poignantly defines the sanctification that is accomplished on our behalf and every aspect of sanctification that grows out of what was accomplished.

### *John 17:17–19*

> Sanctify them in the truth; your word is truth. As you have sent me into the world, so I have sent them into the world. And for their sakes I sanctify myself, so that they also may be sanctified in the truth.

In addition to what was mentioned about this text in reference to 1 Peter 1:22 (chap. 4), Jesus's prayer warrants review and further attention. The means of the disciples' sanctification is the truth, the Word. This is commonly understood as a reference to the Bible—the Word of God written. Certainly Jesus's reference to "your word" has implications for Scripture, though in the overall context of John's Gospel (i.e., the centrality of Jesus as the *logos*) and the immediate context of this discourse, it is more likely a self-reference. Jesus is the Truth, and his self-sanctification constitutes the focal point and end point of the disciples' sanctification.

Richard Bauckham also suggests that this may be "simply a word of appointment and commissioning."[1] In either or both cases Jesus is

1. Bauckham, "The Holiness of Jesus," 112. Bauckham asserts,

> The common translation of ἁγιάζειν in this passage as "sanctify" has probably misled many English readers into supposing that the reference is to a process

the sanctifying One as the Truth and Word of God. As God's Word—God's performative Word—and on behalf of the Father, Jesus set the disciples apart and sent them by that Word.

Thus, this sanctifying act is inherently missional. The "setting apart for divine purpose" aspect of consecration and sanctification quickly returns to view here. Jesus set the stage for this in an earlier part of his discourse (15:3) by assuring them of their cleansing through his word—a central sanctification element—as the condition for their fruitfulness.

Their sanctification depended on Jesus's self-sanctification. He set himself apart for his mission—his "sentness" by the Father (17:18; 20:21). Their "sentness" derived from his "sentness." Additionally, although his sanctification did not need to include cleansing from personal sin (Heb. 4:15), he nevertheless experienced a representative and vicarious cleansing (similar to his baptism)—a vicarious sanctification—that pointed to the cleansing from sin that he would ultimately provide.

By extension, the sanctification of all disciples depends on Jesus's sanctification because he assumed our humanity and made the way—in every conceivable and necessary way—for us to be restored to God. He is the Sanctified One with whom believers are united through the Holy Spirit and, therefore, benefit from a sanctification that is both participative and derived.[2] Bauckham suggests, "It is because Jesus' self-consecration leads him to self-sacrifice on the cross that he does it for the sake of his disciples, 'so that they also may be consecrated in truth' (17:19). By fulfilling the mission for which the Father consecrated him, Jesus makes it possible for his disciples also to be set apart for God's service."[3]

---

of being made ethically holy (since this is the meaning of "sanctification" in traditional Protestant theology). In fact the reference is to an act of God that consecrates the disciples for his service, though it is an act that results in a state of holiness, i.e. of having-been-set-apart for God. . . . But what is the act of consecration? . . . Jesus *asks* God to consecrate them (17:17). The act is still future, as the fact that the consecration of the disciples follows from Jesus' self-consecration to sacrificial death (17:19) requires. (111–12 [emphasis original])

2. Torrance, *Trinitarian Faith*, 167.

3. Bauckham, "The Holiness of Jesus," 110.

***1 Corinthians 1:30***

He is the source of your life in Christ Jesus, who became for us wisdom from God, and righteousness and sanctification and redemption.

As the wisdom of God, contrasting to worldly wisdom, Christ Jesus is now the source of our righteousness, sanctification, and redemption.[4] Here Paul pulls together three aspects of salvation to show the exhaustive and comprehensive nature of salvation through Jesus.[5] Though sanctification is often treated as a consequence or result of justification, as something to be experienced subsequent to and on the basis of justification, Paul believed that it is essential to our salvation and did not acknowledge such sequencing. In the most fundamental sense, Jesus *is* our sanctification.[6] All considerations of sanctification in every other aspect must begin here.

Paul prefaces this soteriologically condensed assertion in a curious manner, equating God's exhaustive work of salvation in Jesus Christ with God's wisdom. Why this link and what are its implications? Gordon Fee explains, "In a community where 'wisdom' was part of a higher spirituality divorced from ethical consequences, Paul says that God has made Christ to become 'wisdom' for us all right, but that means he has made him to become for us the one who redeems from sin and leads to holiness—ethical behavior that is consonant with the gospel."[7] In this instance sanctification is displayed as the living anchor point of salvation.

The moral results and implications of sanctification can be pursued in a healthy and theologically appropriate manner only as they

4. David Peterson contends that *hagiasmos* in this text "is a reference to the work of sanctification mentioned in 1 Corinthians 1:2; 6:11. It is a way of describing the saving work of God in Christ, drawing people into an exclusive relationship with himself through the cross" (*Possessed by God*, 141).

5. Peterson, *Possessed by God*, 44.

6. Strobel, "Sanctified in the Son." Strobel concludes from this text that our sanctification is as final as our justification. This does not blur the distinctive function of justification, nor does it either preclude or trivialize the need and responsibility for transformation. Rather, Strobel insists, transformation is rooted in Jesus Christ the Sanctified One. Such assurance stabilizes the prospect of transformation from the uncertainties and challenges that otherwise would dishearten us and misdirect the process.

7. Fee, *First Epistle to the Corinthians*, 87.

are nourished by conscious attention to this pylon. All that has been accomplished in sanctification is in Jesus Christ. Imperatives related to transformation (to be considered later) essentially insist that we continually live out and live into this sanctification that has been accomplished for us in Jesus Christ. Thus, our lives are conformed to him and his perfect, responsive, trusting relationship with the Father. All eschatological challenges and hopes related to sanctification draw us toward and more deeply into what he already is for us and has done for us.

This christocentric orientation of sanctification provides a practical, concrete focal point for the cultivation of character. Words such as "godliness," "holiness," "blamelessness," and "purity" have specific meaning when located in the person of Jesus Christ and his relationship (vicariously) with the Father. That's good news because our pursuit of those traits is not at the mercy of every notion of virtue or piety that captivates attention in the religious marketplace. Nor does our pursuit of those traits begin with us. The sanctification of Jesus and our sanctification in Jesus rescue us from unclear, anthropocentric notions of sanctification and from unattainable, burdensome forms of piety.

### *1 Peter 3:15*

> But in your hearts sanctify Christ as Lord. Always be ready to make your defense to anyone who demands from you an accounting for the hope that is in you.

Here Peter uses the verb *hagiasate* (ἁγιάσατε) to express the prominence that believers are to give Jesus Christ in their lives. In light of the Roman Empire's pressure to pay homage to Caesar as "Lord," Peter's exhortation carries considerable gravitas. When believers "sanctify Christ as Lord," they rest the weight of their lives on his claim to preeminence over all other powers and authorities, especially those that can have immediate and tangible impact on their physical well-being.

Clearly, as seen in the other instances in this chapter, sanctification here does not refer primarily to change of character, growth, or even cleansing from sin, since it applies to Jesus Christ. This case of sanctification appeals to a particular sense of the "setting apart" that sanctification involves. By implication, the setting apart or sanctification of Jesus Christ as Lord designates the believer's allegiance by distinguishing Christ from all others who would claim it.

## Sanctification of Unbelievers

In 1 Corinthians 7:14 Paul makes a puzzling statement that hardly aligns with conventionally accepted conceptions of sanctification. He argues for the sanctification of unbelieving spouses of believers and of the children of these spiritually mixed marriages without reference to whether the children were believers. Isolated and unusual as this text appears to be, it must be appropriately factored into the doctrinal profile of sanctification. Close examination of Paul's comment shows that this appeal to sanctification actually supports the overall profile in which accomplished sanctification undergirds and defines all other aspects of sanctification.

### *1 Corinthians 7:14*

> For the unbelieving husband is made holy through his wife, and the unbelieving wife is made holy through her husband. Otherwise, your children would be unclean, but as it is, they are holy.

Numerous recent commentators acknowledge the influence of the Corinthian context on Paul's remarks in this passage.[8] His presenting concern was that marriages not be broken simply because they were spiritually mixed, but rather that those marriages reflect God's peace. He apparently thought that some would perceive the marriage (involving sexual intimacy) of a believer to an unbeliever to spiritually contaminate the believer,[9] as would a believer's participation in temple prostitution.

Martin Luther took Paul's comments about the sanctification of unbelieving spouses or children to imply something not about the

8. See, for example, Ciampa and Rosner, *First Letter to the Corinthians*; Fitzmyer, *First Corinthians*; Garland, *1 Corinthians*; Perkins, *First Corinthians*.

9. Fee, *First Epistle to the Corinthians*, 299–300.

spiritual status of those individuals, but about how the believing spouse/parent can live with them without personal spiritual contamination before the Lord. In other words, through the faith of the believer (which sanctifies [Acts 26:18]), the unbelieving spouse/children occupy a sanctified space in the believer's life.[10] Likewise, Roy Ciampa and Brian Rosner affirm that for an unbelieving spouse to have been sanctified "clearly does not mean that they have been saved or now benefit from the covenantal status of the believing spouse, since 7:16 shows that that is an effect that can only be hoped for as the marriage unfolds. And there is no suggestion that it means that such unbelievers experience serious moral transformation upon the conversion of their spouses."[11] With such delimitations, what then did Paul think it meant for the unbelieving spouses and children?

Preben Vang draws attention to the significant communal implications of Paul's sanctification terminology:

> The "Western" question posed runs something like, how can an unbelieving spouse become holy (sanctified) as an individual through a mere relationship with a believer? Translating *hagios* ("holy") in terms of separation rather than belonging, and relating the saying to eternal salvation, many commentators search for an interpretation that explains Paul's saying as a reference to the significance of continuous exposure to the gospel. . . .
>
> This verse [1 Cor. 7:14], however, is probably better understood in cultures with greater appreciation of community. Read in light of God's election of Israel, for example, where the recognition of Israel as God's holy people does not seem to be jeopardized even by the idol worship of some community members, the inclusion of the unbelieving spouse and children in the group of the sanctified becomes understandable. . . . Since one of the spouses by faith has become a member of Christ's community, the whole family is covered by that blessing, and the believer should not seek a divorce. . . . If a spouse

10. See Luther, *Commentaries on 1 Corinthians 7, 1 Corinthians 15*, 35. There he writes, "They [unbelieving children] are not holy in themselves (St. Paul is not discussing *this* holiness) but are holy to you, so that your own holiness may associate with them and raise them without profaning you, just as though they were holy things" (emphasis original).

11. Ciampa and Rosner, *First Letter to the Corinthians*, 297–98.

> becomes a Christian after marriage, God's presence will bless the whole household (cf. Exod. 30:29; Lev. 6:18).
>
> . . . That Paul uses "unclean" (*akathartos*) as his antonym to "holy" (*hagios*) places his discussion in the realm of spiritual powers, but not as a statement on eternal salvation. Christ's holy presence overpowers the realm of uncleanness, not vice versa.[12]

Joseph Fitzmyer concurs that sanctification here provides a particular type of ambience that is marked by the presence and the blessing of God, which now define the household spiritually: "So the children too share their parents' holiness, because they are remotely part of the Christian community, even though their mother or father might not be a believer. Thus they 'now' (*nyn de*) benefit also from the spiritual milieu in which they live and grow up, because God's sanctifying power is greater than any unbelief. They are *hagia*, because they share somehow in the consecration expressed by *hegiastai* of v. 14b."[13]

Paul considered this new, sanctified milieu a possible source of spiritual influence on the unbelievers in the household (7:16), presumably as unbelieving spouses and children routinely encounter the reality of the risen Christ and may be persuaded of the truth of the gospel through the presence of God in the life of the believing spouse. Gordon Fee sees the unbelieving spouse and children as "set apart in a special way that hopefully will lead to their salvation."[14]

This potential spiritual influence of sanctification may have been secondary in Paul's mind to the communal realm of divine presence and blessing, as Vang suggests.[15] Otherwise, this sanctification would be provisional or contingent on the conversion of the unbelieving spouse and/or children. Still, though secondary and derivative, the

12. Vang, *1 Corinthians*, 103–4.
13. Fitzmyer, *First Corinthians*, 301.
14. Fee, *First Epistle to the Corinthians*, 301.
15. Karl Barth affirms this order of emphasis in this text. He claims that Paul "obviously reckons with an actual sanctifying power which men can exercise over their neighbours by the simple fact of their existence and presence as Christians. He is not speaking of what Christians must do in this position. Nor is he speaking of how others will react to the fact that Christians are among them with this degree of influence" (*Church Dogmatics*, III/4, 278).

potential for spiritual influence—the missional implications—of sanctification does exist.[16] Through sanctification, God's presence is God's power to effect God's purposes.[17]

Thus, Paul's "odd" reference to the sanctification of unbelievers turns out to be consistent with the sanctification motifs that run through redemptive history. Unbelievers who are married to or who are children of believers enjoy a proximity to the presence and blessing of God, both through the sanctification of their Christian spouse or parent and through that believer's connection to the covenant community that the Spirit of God inhabits. They come close to the real presence of the Triune God. As seen throughout our study thus far, nothing makes change more possible or more likely than the presence of God.

## Sanctification of the Inanimate

Equally enigmatic but laden with sanctification implications is Paul's reference to the holiness of the inanimate realm—that is, food and drink.

### *1 Timothy 4:3–5*

> They forbid marriage and demand abstinence from foods, which God created to be received with thanksgiving by those who believe and know the truth. For everything created by God is good, and nothing is to be rejected, provided it is received with thanksgiving; for it is sanctified by God's word and by prayer.

Sanctification (consecration) of the inanimate is actually not new or unusual, as it can be traced all the way back to Exodus 3:5, where

16. Gary W. Deddo draws on Barth here to underscore how the presence of God through sanctification can be powerfully manifest through parental presence: "Their [believing parents'] very presence with them calls their children towards acknowledging and participating in a reconciled and redeemed relationship with God" (*Karl Barth's Theology of Relations*, 2:244).

17. Fee writes, "Thus in both cases Paul is setting forth a high view of the grace of God at work through the believer toward members of his/her own household (cf. 1 Pet. 3:1)" (*First Epistle to the Corinthians*, 302).

God declared "holy" the patch of ground on which Moses stood in front of the burning bush. Subsequently, the Israelites consecrated various gifts that they offered to the Lord (Exod. 28:38). Consecration was performed for the priest's garments, the altar, the furnishings and utensils used in the holy place, and the bread consumed by the priest in the holy place. Everything, as well as every person in immediate proximity to God's presence and to be used for God's purposes, was to be consecrated. In light of the widespread tendency to understand sanctification first and primarily in terms of personal spiritual maturity and character development, sanctification of the inanimate raises questions that sharpen our understanding of the dominant purpose of sanctification and what actually happens in sanctification.

What is the nature of this sanctification? What happens in this "making holy" of inanimate items such as food and drink, especially in Paul's situation where these were not used in any special cultic or ecclesial manner, as occurred in the tabernacle? Certainly the properties of these ordinary items do not undergo alteration.[18] What changes when those objects become holy? Philip Towner notes, "The root of this is the idea that things or people are brought within the sphere of God's presence or influence."[19] The chemical composition of the dirt under Moses's feet was the same as that of the dirt some distance away. Each object remains what it is. Yet, it serves a different purpose by being brought into the realm of God's presence, that purpose being to serve as the occasion for interaction with and response to the Living God.

Paul insists to the Christians in Ephesus, contra those who sought to enforce unwarranted religious scruples regarding marriage and diet, that God's gifts from creation can be considered holy in their relation to the presence and purposes of God. But how, specifically, does this happen? The Word of God and prayer are primarily instrumental. Towner acknowledges some ambiguity about what Paul had in mind here but considers it likely that "God's word" refers to "what

18. Admittedly, Roman Catholic sacramental theology affirms such change of properties in the eucharistic elements through transubstantiation. I will not engage that argument here, as it is beyond the scope of this study.

19. Towner, *Letters to Timothy and Titus*, 298.

God has declared to be true"[20] about the value of food as God's gift and that "prayer" refers to thanksgiving for the provisions.

Samuel Ngewa suggests a similar interpretation of how God's Word and prayer bring about something holy and new even for food and drink:

> Some speak as if this thanksgiving has a magical property to it. . . . This approach fits with the African traditional belief that a word said by a powerful person or an object set aside by a person in contact with the spiritual world possesses magical power. However, the scriptural position is that all things are at the disposal of our God, to use as he pleases. . . . When God uses an object to achieve his purpose (for example, Paul's handkerchiefs and aprons—Acts 19:12) it would be a mistake to confuse his use of the object with the power the thing itself has. It has power only as long as God chooses to use it for a particular purpose.
>
> Our prayer of gratitude, therefore, does not make the food good. All it does is confirm the goodness that the food already has. . . .
>
> Our food is consecrated not only by prayer but also by *the word of God* (4:5). What does this mean? . . . While it is not possible to be dogmatic on this point, it makes good sense to see the word of God here as Scripture read at the table. Acknowledging that God made food for our use and thanking him for providing it is all that is needed to fulfil all righteousness in matters of food—so long as the food is rightly acquired, does not cause anyone to stumble, and it is good for our health.
>
> God made food good, and our prayer of gratitude confirms its goodness.[21]

A parallel emphasis is found in God's statement to Peter about foods being clean simply because God called them clean (Acts 10:15). The unclean foods that God declared clean represented the gentiles whom God would accept into God's family, as marked by giving them God's own presence through the Holy Spirit (Acts 10:47). Both instances serve as reminders of the performative character of God's Word. With regard to sanctification, God's performative Word of declaration about holiness

20. Towner, *Letters to Timothy and Titus*, 299.
21. Ngewa, *1 & 2 Timothy and Titus*, 91–92 (emphasis original).

is far more than a descriptive act. It actively—powerfully—brings about the newness of which it speaks. In bringing about this newness, other new realities emerge. In the case of Peter and the gentiles, sanctification of the inanimate effected relational change.

When in gratitude we recognize even our daily sustenance as God's gift and invoke God's blessing on it, it becomes an occasion for us to recognize and respond to God's presence and blessing. It nourishes us to serve the Lord, to engage and fulfill God's purposes. It is holy.[22] Extending Paul's argument, we can infer a theology of sanctification for potentially all of life when it is seen and received as God's gift, then offered up to God for his glory and purposes. All of life can indeed be sacred in this manner.

## Conclusion

Jesus's sanctification of himself—setting himself apart for his unique role in the Father's purposes—charts the course for our understanding of all of his disciples' sanctification. We are powerfully set apart and commissioned by God's Word—God's Truth. Jesus is that Word, that Truth, in whom we have new life, covenantal belonging, and mission. This changes us as we submit ourselves in obedient pursuit of all that it entails.

Paul's treatment of unbelievers as sanctified through a relationship to a believing spouse or parents forces us to look more deeply into what actually happens in sanctification and why it is so powerful. The unbelievers Paul had in mind were graced with a unique proximity to God's presence through those relationships. God's presence and purposes blessed those marriages and families through the life of the believing spouse or parent, even though the personal eternal destinies of the unbelievers in view were unknown.

Even ordinary objects such as daily food and drink are sanctified—made holy—by the power of God's Word and by grateful response to

22. This realization gave me new appreciation of a common, ritual meal prayer that I have heard almost my entire life, including from my own father: "Lord, bless this food to the nourishment of our bodies and our bodies to your service." There is far more good sanctification theology reflected here than I ever realized.

God. Thus, the ordinary (especially significant if it is not particularly tasty!) becomes the occasion for interaction with the Living God—for worship! The sanctifying Word of God and presence of God effect and compel change. We can and must be transformed as a result of having been sanctified. Accomplished sanctification is powerful—life altering.

# 6

# Sanctification as Liberated Responsibilities and Compelling Promises

The New Testament portrayal of sanctification extends the Old Testament trajectory of consecration in a threefold manner: accomplished, imperatival, and yet to be completed. The accomplished work of God in sanctification has clear ethical implications expressed in bold imperatives and with the anticipation/promise that believers will experience in the future the fullness of all that sanctification provides. We now can explore those texts for what they do and do not say or imply, particularly in the light of what has already been accomplished in sanctification.

The light of accomplished sanctification illuminates imperatives as liberated responsibilities and the yet-to-be-completed aspect of sanctification as compelling promises. This picture is essential in order for us to see the practical implications of reconfiguring the three strands of the doctrine of sanctification and for transformation texts to play their proper role.

## Sanctification Imperatives

Imperatives related to holiness play a dominant role in sanctification discussions and literature. How is that role to be understood in relation to what has already been accomplished? Is the traditional indicative–imperative formulation adequate to account for what occurs in the interplay between these aspects? Can we simply affirm both aspects with the familiar "both . . . and," yet without probing further into their relationship? Does the term "progressive sanctification" adequately and accurately portray the character of the imperatives? These questions will guide our consideration of key, representative texts, beginning with imperatives.

### *Romans 6:19*

> I am speaking in human terms, because of your natural limitations. For just as you once presented your members as slaves to impurity and to greater and greater iniquity, so now present your members as slaves to righteousness for sanctification.

Here Paul provides what could be one of the strongest evidences that sanctification is progressive and meant to increase. Yet, that question turns on the meaning and implications of "slaves to righteousness *for* [or *leading to* (ESV)] sanctification" (*eis hagiasmon*, εἰς ἁγιασμόν). Does that phrase point to a process of personal development such as is conveyed by the notion of transformation?

Both C. E. B. Cranfield and Douglas Moo take it to imply process. Yet, on close examination, both of their arguments are far from conclusive. Cranfield simply asserts, without explanation or warrant, that process is in view and that *hagiasmon* is better translated as "sanctification" rather than either "holiness" or "consecration." His rationale for implying that "sanctification" is somehow distinct from "holiness" or "consecration" is unclear. He assumes that in referring to sanctification, Paul had "ethical renewal" in mind.[1] However, "ethical renewal" is not synonymous with the sort of cumulative or progressive character development so frequently associated with

1. Cranfield, *Epistle to the Romans*, 1:327.

sanctification. Ethical renewal is more easily understood simply as behavioral change in light of the reality of sanctification.

Moo contends, "'Sanctification' may refer to the state of 'holiness,' as the end product of a life of living in service of righteousness. But most of Paul's uses of this word have an active connotation: the *process* of 'becoming holy.' This is probably the case here also."[2] In his footnote to this point, Moo cites as support 1 Thessalonians 4:3, 4, 7 and 1 Timothy 2:15, claiming that 1 Corinthians 1:30 and 2 Thessalonians 2:13 "are not clear." Yet, the active sense of the word in 1 Thessalonians 4 and in 1 Timothy 2 does not necessarily imply progressive growth but simply active holy living. First Corinthians 1:30 speaks of Jesus Christ having become our holiness. Second Thessalonians 2:13 speaks of the Spirit's sanctifying work in relation to our salvation.

It is unclear what Moo finds unclear about those passages, unless it is how they could imply process. An "active connotation" most simply implies activity—practice. The inference of a gradually increasing or accumulating process represents more of an assumption than the obvious reading of the text. Moo's initial concession that it "may refer to the state of holiness, as the end product of a life of living in service of righteousness" actually stands as the most straightforward reading of the text, especially when examined in the light of the overall patterns of usage in Scripture.

Does holiness increase in some sense, just as the wickedness to which Paul contrasted it appears to increase? Clearly, Paul called these believers to pursue a course of life that follows the trajectory of righteousness in order to fulfill all the implications of being holy people. His comments leading up to verse 19 help clarify the point. In the immediately preceding context he calls them to a process of obedience: "Therefore, do not let sin exercise dominion in your mortal bodies, to make you obey their passions" (v. 12); "No longer present your members to sin as instruments of wickedness, but present yourselves to God as those who have been brought from death to life, and present your members to God as instruments of righteousness" (v. 13).

2. Moo, *Epistle to the Romans*, 405.

In keeping with these imperatives, Paul's language in verse 16 suggests that the process is one of submission, either to sin or to God and righteousness. The process in either direction has a specific, inherent outcome: wickedness or righteousness. Wickedness and righteousness can increase in two obvious senses: more acts or manifestations in either realm and more bondage to either realm.

Along this line, Victor Paul Furnish points out the clarification added by verse 22, where Paul says, "But now that you have been freed from sin and enslaved to God, the advantage you get is sanctification. The end is eternal life." This statement clarifies parallels that Paul employs in this overall argument: "God" and "righteousness" in verses 13 and 19, and again in verses 20 and 22.[3] "This is even more striking," Furnish observes, "when comparing verses 13 (surrender to God means righteousness) and 22 (slavery to God means sanctification)."[4] Thus, he argues that Paul's focus in this text was the effects of repeated acts in either direction—toward sin, resulting in slavery, or toward God, resulting in sanctification.

Furnish argues that "the RSV translation of the first phrase [in v. 19b] is misleading ('to impurity and *to greater and greater iniquity*')," as it inappropriately implies "successively more serious stages of iniquity" that then fosters the parallel assumption that εἰς ἁγιασμόν "could be taken in the same way, yielding the idea that sanctification is the highest level of righteousness."[5] Sanctification, in Paul's argument here, "has to do with the service of righteousness, 'slavery' to it (v. 18)—which means, to God (v. 22)."[6] In keeping with the trajectory and ethos of sanctification established thus far, sanctification here focuses on submitting to and serving God rather than on the process of developing or accruing greater levels of personal character. Furnish writes, "Righteousness is not the goal of obedience but its presupposition."[7]

Without question, there is increase in view in this text. The process of submission to God's righteousness increasingly leads to a life

3. Furnish, *Theology and Ethics in Paul*, 156.
4. Furnish, *Theology and Ethics in Paul*, 156.
5. Furnish, *Theology and Ethics in Paul*, 157 (emphasis original).
6. Furnish, *Theology and Ethics in Paul*, 157.
7. Furnish, *Theology and Ethics in Paul*, 196.

that reflects a forgiven and cleansed heart before God. It increasingly fosters responsiveness to the presence of God through the Spirit. Yet submission to and engagement with God's purposes carries the weight of the argument. Growth and transformation are definitely related to sanctification as responses to the imperatives, but, on careful examination, they are not the focus of the increase.

Exegesis of texts such as Romans 6:19 frequently focuses on personal growth, assuming overlap between sanctification and transformation that those texts will not support. In this text, the process of submission to righteousness (to God) implies, at the very least, the end goal of holy living but most prominently places believers into service for God's righteous purposes. Nothing more needs to be added and nothing is lost without additional assumptions about process.

### *Romans 12:1–2*

> I appeal to you therefore, brothers and sisters, by the mercies of God, to present your bodies as a living sacrifice, holy and acceptable to God, which is your spiritual worship. Do not be conformed to this world, but be transformed by the renewing of your minds, so that you may discern what is the will of God—what is good and acceptable and perfect.

In treatments of sanctification, both academic and popular, this text routinely appears to support the notion of progressive sanctification. The imperative is actually directed not at sanctification but rather at the nature of submission to God and at transformation. "Holy" (*hagian*, ἁγίαν) functions adjectivally along with "pleasing" (*euareston*, εὐάρεστον) in verse 1 to qualify the "living sacrifice"[8] that we are to offer to God. Assumptions about sanctification often imported into this text seem to be derived from what Paul says about transformation in verse 2. Setting those assumptions aside for the moment, what specific role does sanctification actually play in this text?

Richard Longenecker presents it succinctly. These "adjectives signal that Christians are to present themselves to God as those (1) who are committed entirely to his purposes, (2) who accept at all times his continued cleansing of their lives, and (3) who endeavor always to

8. Longenecker, *Epistle to the Romans*, 920.

act in ways that are consistent with his will."[9] Longenecker captures an important and positive feature of the linkage between sanctification and transformation: sanctification constitutes a precondition for transformation.

Believers can be transformed in the particular christologically defined manner that Paul had in mind only as they present themselves to God for cleansing from sin (cf. 1 John 1:9) and devote/submit/entrust themselves to God's purposes. Implicit in this devotion is the response to God's covenantal love and commitment that underpinned consecration in the Old Testament. Transformation depends on what has been done for the believer in sanctification—the cleansing, the communion with God, the setting apart—accomplished in Christ and by the Spirit. Later we will explore further the transformative aspect of this imperative and how sanctification gives transformation its unique character.

### *2 Corinthians 7:1*

> Since we have these promises, beloved, let us cleanse ourselves from every defilement of body and of spirit, making holiness perfect in the fear of God.

With the phrase "making holiness perfect," did Paul envision holiness as progressively increasing? He uses a first-person plural exhortation—"let us cleanse ourselves"—to set before the Corinthian believers the same purification that Peter recognized as having occurred in the believers whom he addressed (1 Pet. 1:22) and to which John appealed (1 John 1:7). Each instance draws on the same word group—*katharos* (καθαρός). This hortatory appeal functions as the primary imperative, while "making holiness perfect in the fear of God" either serves to qualify or serves as the second of a two-pronged imperative. In what sense, then, is holiness made perfect?

The participle "making . . . perfect" (*epitelountes*, ἐπιτελοῦντες) has commonly been assumed to teach that sanctification increases—that is, the notion of progressive sanctification.[10] However, even with

9. Longenecker, *Epistle to the Romans*, 920.
10. See, for example, Harris, *Second Epistle to the Corinthians*, 513–15.

the imperatival force of the overall construction, that theological interpretation has not proven to be uniformly convincing. According to Linda Belleville, "The sense is not immediately clear. . . . The participle (*epitelountes*) may well define the result of the action of cleansing (*let us purify ourselves . . . perfecting holiness*). Looked at this way, holiness becomes a reality as we purify ourselves from physical and spiritual pollutants."[11] Paul Barnett extends this line of argument even further by pointing to the church as indwelt by the Spirit and to the implications of the Spirit's sanctifying presence for the church:

> The verb "perfect," meaning "complete" or "fulfill," is a present participle that . . . probably does not imply a process of perfection in moral holiness. The holiness is covenantal rather than developmental or processive in character. On the contrary, the action of separation from the idol-worshiping cults (v. 17), which is tantamount to the act of self-cleansing from defilement (v. 1a), should be seen as a prerequisite to the perfection of the church's calling to be God's holy temple (v. 16); without this separation the Corinthians cannot be what they are called to be. To infer a theology of moral and spiritual development at this point, although taught elsewhere (see on 3:18), would be to import a theme that is foreign to the present context.[12]

David Garland arrives at a similar conclusion in light of Paul's overall flow of thought in this letter: "We can compare this command with 1 Corinthians 6:10–11. God has cleansed them, but this cleansing is for naught if they persist in defiling associations."[13] He continues, "Purifying themselves and perfecting their holiness would mean, in this context, withdrawing from any unholy alliances and association with idolatry."[14] Consistent with the pattern observed in the Old Testament, sanctification has clear implications for ethical obedience. The subtle, though important, distinction is that sanctification itself does not increase while ethical obedience can and must increase.

11. Belleville, *2 Corinthians*, 185–86.
12. Barnett, *Second Epistle to the Corinthians*, 357.
13. Garland, *1 Corinthians*, 341–42.
14. Garland, *1 Corinthians*, 343.

While a theology of spiritual progress or transformation enjoys ample biblical support (which we will consider in chaps. 8 and 9), the task of realigning the doctrine of sanctification with biblical proportions demands properly relating sanctification to transformation, not assuming that they are synonymous.

This involves clarification of what the imperatival texts actually say and caution against importing theological assumptions from one text or text group into another. As Garland indicates, the process enjoined in texts such as this can be better understood in light of the cultural and textual context as referring to a set of acts by which believers were increasingly to enact with integrity their holy identity as God's people—God's temple.

#### *1 Thessalonians 4:3–7*

> For this is the will of God, your sanctification: that you abstain from fornication; that each one of you know how to control your own body in holiness and honor, not with lustful passion, like the Gentiles who do not know God; that no one wrong or exploit a brother or sister in this matter, because the Lord is an avenger in all these things, just as we have already told you beforehand and solemnly warned you. For God did not call us to impurity but in holiness.

For Paul to say here that God wants us to be sanctified has commonly been understood as God's desire that we grow. Without doubt, God does intend for us to grow, as plenty of other texts demonstrate. Yet here that does not appear to be the central issue that Paul had in mind. Nijay Gupta offers important background to Paul's remarks: "When he [Paul] originally instructed them, he shared not simply the good-news message, but also counsel regarding 'how you must walk and live to please God.' We sometimes call this 'ethics,' but Paul would not have seen a distinction between 'theology' and 'ethics.' For Paul, the free gift of new life in Messiah Jesus automatically entails a new set of personal and social standards under the Lordship of Jesus."[15]

Notice the similarity with what Paul enjoins in Philippians 1:27: "Live your life in a manner worthy of the gospel of Christ." The

15. Gupta, *1–2 Thessalonians*, 78.

gospel, for Paul, encompassed God's redemptive work and contained its own ethical contours that the church must identify and follow in each time and setting. Gupta continues,

> He goes on . . . to refer in quite specific terms to the nature of the will of God. God wishes, in particular, that they are "consecrated" to him (*hagiasmos*). To be consecrated is to be dedicated to holiness. Here Paul views holiness as a kind of maintained condition of purity and personal dedication to God. Sometimes this word is explained as if it were simply about *not* doing something (i.e., avoiding worldliness), and Paul does point out here what jeopardizes holiness. However, the language of holiness in Jewish thought has an important *positive* value. Holiness involves being close to God and being available and dedicated to serving God wholeheartedly.[16]

Abraham Malherbe points out from the immediate context that Paul's focus on specific behavior defines sanctification in this text: "Paul's exhortation in verse 1, that his readers engage in conduct that is required to please God, is given specificity by these infinitives, which have the force of imperatives. Sanctification therefore requires human effort. In the second bracket (v. 7), however, *hagiasmos* describes God's action."[17] The "human effort" that sanctification requires is the effort to fulfill the imperatival implications of sanctification. Without the Spirit's presence (v. 8), such behavioral imperatives would be moralistic. As we have seen, the Spirit's presence is as crucial to sanctification as are particular ways of obedience to God.

This text also points to the identity created by sanctification. Jeffrey Weima notes, "The holiness that previously has been the exclusive privilege and calling of Israel has now also become God's purpose for Gentiles at Thessalonica who have 'turned to God from idols to serve a true and living God' (1:9). The holiness that has previously been the characteristic distinguishing Israel from the Gentile nations has now also become the boundary marker that separates the Thessalonian Gentile believers from 'the Gentiles who do not know God' (4:5)."[18]

16. Gupta, *1–2 Thessalonians*, 78.
17. Malherbe, *Letters to the Thessalonians*, 225.
18. Weima, *1–2 Thessalonians*, 265.

In verse 7 Paul may seem simply to repeat himself, but the Greek construction for "but in holiness" (*all' en hagiasmō*, ἀλλ' ἐν ἁγιασμῷ) highlights holiness as the domain of life that contrasts with the realm of worldly inclinations. Charles Wanamaker comments, "The Thessalonians were called 'into the sphere where God's sanctification takes place.' This picks up the theme of 4:3. The emphasis, however, is not on the readers' need to strive for sanctification but rather on the fact that Christian experience is to be lived in the sphere of God's holiness."[19]

Weima makes a similar suggestion: "If Paul here in 1 Thessalonians 4:7 similarly is referring to the state or condition of the Thessalonians at their calling, his point is that holiness is not so much a future goal as a past and present reality—a state of holiness that started already at their conversion and continues in their current lives."[20] Weima offers a valid interpretive option that shifts the focus of holiness from an experiential process to the divine character and relationship that orient believers' practice.

#### *Hebrews 12:14*

> Pursue peace with everyone, and the holiness without which no one will see the Lord.

In what sense is holiness to be "pursued" (*diōkete*, διώκετε)? Does this pursuit imply a striving that contributes to the increase or accumulation of holiness in a person's character? What assumptions about the nature of holiness are implied in the warning that holiness is a prerequisite to seeing God? This warning, ironically, has often disturbed if not crippled the assurance of those who are most intent on the pursuit of holiness.

What the NIV translates as an infinitive—"to be holy"—may seem to imply a process, but actually it is a simple noun, "holiness" (*hagiasmon*, ἁγιασμόν), the direct object of *diōkete*, "pursue." The NRSV translation, "Pursue . . . holiness," reflects the undiluted, straightforward force and significance of the imperative. Clearly, God's holiness

19. Wanamaker, *Epistles to the Thessalonians*, 157.
20. Weima, *1–2 Thessalonians*, 280.

places demands on those who would be in relationship with God both temporally and in eternity. Holiness entails specific acts of obedience, defined by God's holiness as outlined in God's covenant relations and embodied in Jesus Christ,[21] and calling for an unqualified, unencumbered, active, trusting response. However, do even our best efforts cause holiness to grow in our character in ways that qualify us to meet God?

If this holiness refers primarily to purity of heart or personal character relative to God's holy nature, then the equation is set up for perpetual failure and frustration. On our best days, we know that we fall woefully short of God's holiness. This phenomenon gives rise to the widespread affirmation, often expressed in the Reformed tradition, that the more one desires holiness and grows in holiness the more painfully is one aware of the lack of holiness.

J. I. Packer expresses this sentiment with the pithy notion of "reach exceeding grasp." "Discerning sinful desires in themselves despite their longing to be sin-free, and finding that in their quest for total righteousness their reach exceeds their grasp, they will live in tension and distress at their frustrating infirmities (cf. Rom. 7:14–25)."[22] As accurate as Packer's observation may be from an experiential standpoint, it is questionable whether Hebrews 12:14 contributes to that conclusion. Though Packer and others in the Reformed tradition are quick to highlight justification and the grace and promises of God as the basis for the believer's assurance, the assertions seem to work against each other experientially, leaving the serious believer in more, rather than less, of an existential conundrum.

Harold Attridge suggests an alternative way forward, one that pays even closer attention to the language of the text and points to a primarily communal, rather than individual, focus of the imperative:

> The linkage of inner communal peace with the cultic notion of sanctity is of some significance and the two terms serve to specify one another. In what follows, Hebrews will specifically refer to the ultimate basis of the community's holiness, the sacrifice of Christ

21. See the excellent treatment of the covenantal character of this holiness in Allen, *Sanctification*.

22. Packer, "Evangelical Foundations of Spirituality," 2:265.

> (13:12). From the character of that event certain implications flow, both for personal conduct and for the appropriate response in worship. Communal "peace," in the broadest sense, is rooted in, and is the fullest expression of, the holiness of the community gathered around Christ's "altar." Apart from such sanctification . . . no one will "see the Lord."[23]

Communal responsibility always consists of personal or individual responsibility. Pitting them against each other results in a false dilemma. Attridge anchors the imperative in the accomplished holiness that the writer has taken pains to explain and defend throughout the epistle. The holiness that we must have in order to see the Lord has been provided by the Lord. Every bit as important, Attridge sees the writer attributing this accomplished holiness to the community. The holiness to be pursued is the holiness that has been given to the church through Jesus Christ. Believers are left then with the simultaneous freedom and responsibility to live that out, or live into it, as suggested by the preceding verse (v. 13), which quotes Proverbs 4:26, urging people to stay on the path.

### *1 Peter 1:14–16*

> Like obedient children, do not be conformed to the desires that you formerly had in ignorance. Instead, as he who called you is holy, be holy yourselves in all your conduct; for it is written, "You shall be holy, for I am holy."

Perhaps as much as any other New Testament text, Peter's straightforward exhortation to be holy has served as a container for assumptions about sanctification. It is vital to remember that the same word group—*hagios* (ἅγιος)—lies behind the translation of both "holiness" and "sanctification." This is crucial because the differences in how the word group has been translated in various texts have contributed to the variety of perceptions about what holiness or sanctification mean. Peter's words here come with bracing intensity, conveying the seriousness of the call to holiness.

23. Attridge, *Epistle to the Hebrews*, 367.

Many versions translate *hagios* here as "holy." As a clarifying exercise, replace "holy" with "sanctified" in each place, and then see how it reads. For example, "Instead, as he who called you is sanctified, so be sanctified yourselves in all your conduct; for it is written: 'You shall be sanctified, because I am sanctified.'" That rendering will sound odd to many, but it is every bit as valid as using "holy" and forces us to think more deeply about what Peter was saying. Certainly, God does not need to be purified or cleansed as we do, so we are not sanctified (or holy) in exactly the same sense as God is. Yet, our sanctification derives from and reflects God's holiness. Jesus's sanctification was for the sake of our sanctification (John 17:19).

The call here is actually rather simple when considered in its context. The command to pursue holiness in conduct is prefaced by the simple imperative not to conform to evil desires. Here, as in Paul's letters, the background of the imperative is the temptation and tendency of believers to resort to the practices and allegiances of their pagan backgrounds. Peter Davids underscores this feature of holiness, stating, "The first description of their obedience here is negative: they are not to return to their former pagan life-style." He goes on to say, "The calling is a calling to God and therefore to separation from the way of life of this age (cf. Eph. 4:1; 1 Thess. 4:7)."[24]

John Elliott pulls together important features from the context of Peter's letter: "This holiness of the believers is a result of their election by God (1:1; 2:4–10; 5:13), their sanctification by the Holy Spirit (1:2), their call by God, the Holy One (1:15), and their redemption through the blood of Christ, the holy lamb (1:18–19; 1:2c)."[25] Without a doubt, as Elliott goes on to emphasize, the holiness that Peter envisions relates to their conduct—conduct in keeping with the character of God. Conduct and maturity/growth, though related, are not synonymous. Karen Jobes equates holiness with alignment of "thinking and behavior to God's character" as "first revealed through the covenant God made with the people he had chosen for himself."[26]

24. Davids, *First Epistle of Peter*, 67, 69.

25. Elliott, *1 Peter*, 362.

26. Jobes, *1 Peter*, 112. Jobes brings the transformation theme into view. "In terms of moral transformation, the goal of both the old and the new covenants is the same—to create a people who morally conform to God's character" (113). To see

Peter seems to have had foremost in mind specific practices and commitments on both sides of the moral ledger. Certainly he expected growth and transformation to occur so that godly behaviors (covenantally prescribed and contextually appropriate) were increasingly internalized and habituated. Yet, a proper understanding and appreciation of this particular call to sanctification demands that we see it as Peter saw it—in light of God's calling and election, the role and presence of the Holy Spirit, and the work of Christ.

John Oswalt summarizes four key features of holiness from this passage: "(1) Holiness first of all defines a way of behaving; (2) It is a way of behaving which is determined by the character of God; (3) It is a way of behaving which all Christians are expected to manifest; and (4) It is a way of behaving which is markedly different from that of unbelievers."[27] Peter's straightforward call reflects the fact that holiness always has implications for conduct—conduct that reflects God's character.

Although the imperatival dimensions of holiness are deeply familiar—perhaps overly familiar—to many, they are not always properly distinguished from and related to concepts such as transformation, growth, and maturity, which depend on sanctification but are not identical with it. Blurring the imperatives and transformation and then resting the blurred composite on an underdeveloped theology of accomplished sanctification have fostered confusing and toxic results downstream, which will receive our attention in part 3.

This section on New Testament sanctification imperatives, while selective, reflects the particular force of those imperatives. Some may feel uneasy about these imperatives from fear that they can easily lead to a legalistic and moralistic tone in the Christian life. Perhaps some of those fears have been fostered more by negative personal experiences than by the texts of Scripture. At any rate, in order to

---

moral transformation in texts such as this is quite common and part of what I'm attempting to clarify in this book. This is not at all to dismiss transformation, since the New Testament provides and we still need a robust theology of transformation. It is simply to avoid importing into sanctification texts more than is really there and to establish the framework in which sanctification and transformation can be properly related. The two biblical concepts are related, though not identical.

27. Oswalt, *Called to Be Holy*, 2.

avoid the trap of legalism and moralism, the biblical imperatives sadly fall prey to so many qualifications as to dilute and circumvent their necessary force.

However, the force of these imperatives need not be diluted if they are seen in proper relationship to the accomplished aspect of sanctification. They can and should be seen for what they are and faced with courageous responsiveness as part of a healthy spiritual life. When properly grounded and focused, sanctification/holiness imperatives are no longer haunted by the specter of legalism and moralism.

## Sanctification Yet to Be Completed

The third category of sanctification texts points to a future or eschatological dimension, some sense in which sanctification is yet to be completed. These texts, in combination with sanctification imperatives, often create the impression that sanctification must grow in the life of the believer and is more contingent than accomplished. The power and significance of God's sanctifying act through Christ and the Spirit can easily be overshadowed apart from a clear understanding of what still lays ahead in sanctification.

The crucial question is the sense in which sanctification is yet to be completed. As with the imperatives, it is crucial not to read these texts with assumptions about progression that are not clearly substantiated (e.g., by texts examined in the previous section of this chapter) and then read more in this future dimension than its grounding in accomplished sanctification will sustain. The past, present, and future aspects of sanctification are not simply discrete theological compartments that sit adjacent to one another, equally proportioned on a flat conceptual grid. Rather, they are organically and dynamically related such that what God has already accomplished sets the trajectory, defines the telos, and provides the content for the present and the future of sanctification. In light of what has been considered so far, what does the future aspect of sanctification involve?

All that God does in our sanctification is tethered eschatologically in the promise of standing before the Lord and of then inhabiting a new world—a world that in its entirety, and in ways proper to it, has been made into (including purging or cleansing [2 Pet. 3:7–13]) the kind of world (the "holy city, the new Jerusalem") where God is pleased to dwell with us (Rev. 21:2–3). Three representative texts will illustrate what is often considered a future culmination of sanctification. The image of standing before the Lord appears in each of the texts, and in one of them, 1 Thessalonians 3:13, standing before the Lord is directly connected to his return.

- **Ephesians 1:4:** "Just as he chose us in Christ before the foundation of the world to be holy and blameless before him in love."
- **Colossians 1:22:** "He has now reconciled [you] in his fleshly body through death, so as to present you holy and blameless and irreproachable before him."
- **1 Thessalonians 3:13:** "And may he so strengthen your hearts in holiness that you may be blameless before our God and Father at the coming of our Lord Jesus with all his saints."

These Pauline texts convey the same basic emphasis: righteous conduct. Andrew Lincoln sees Ephesians 1:4 as Paul's summary of God's overall sanctifying work in the church, with blamelessness and love as positive expressions of holiness and "absence of moral defect or sin" as the negative aspect.[28] Lynn Cohick views holiness here in reference to present conduct: "In 1:4 a strong case can be made that holiness and blamelessness are the character traits that Christians should exhibit, to God's glory."[29] Here and in 4:24 Paul cryptically stated holiness as God's intention for us.[30]

The focus in Ephesians 1:4 is not on holiness as a contingent or progressively culminating phenomenon but, in a more punctiliar sense,

28. Lincoln, *Ephesians*, 24.

29. Cohick, *Ephesians*, 48.

30. Technically, 4:24 is not a sanctification text in the same sense because in that verse "holiness" (*hosiotēs*, ὁσιότης) translates a word from outside the *hagios* (ἅγιος) word group. Clinton Arnold states, "The distinguishing features of the new self that Paul identifies here are 'righteousness and holiness (δικαιοσύνη and ὁσιότης).' These two terms appear together commonly to summarize a virtuous life that is obedient to the commands of God." He continues, "The term 'holiness' (ὁσιότης), when used by itself, often has the sense of a proper attitude toward God. It is also used in local inscriptions to refer to a proper piety toward the gods" (*Ephesians*, 290).

on the result of God's promise and work to fit the covenant people for God's presence. Clinton Arnold, though retaining the traditional assumption that holiness is a process, concedes that "based on the work of Christ on the cross, believers have already been bestowed with holiness. He [Paul] thus refers to believers as 'holy ones' nine times in this letter (see 1:1, 15, 18; 2:19; 3:8, 18; 4:12; 5:3; 6:18)."[31]

The yet-to-be-completed holiness is the promise that God will bring people into full integrity with who they have been chosen and made to be in Christ. Sin will no longer mark their existence. Not without significance is that in Paul's mind the eschatological dimension of sanctification has an ecclesial character, which should not be overlooked by the Western tendency toward individualism.

Similarly, Colossians 1:22 refers to how, through Christ, believers presently stand before God holy, blameless, and free from accusation. The holiness that Paul has in mind here is not entirely in the future, though it has future implications when he goes on to say in verse 23, "provided that you continue securely established and steadfast in the faith, without shifting from the hope promised by the gospel." Although Arminians and Calvinists may move from this statement into discussions of whether Paul admitted of contingency in salvation, Paul intended to highlight the experiential implications and responsibilities of being holy people. Holiness given must be holiness lived.

First Thessalonians 3:13 raises an important question: How does the strengthening of our hearts relate to holiness? Clues lay in Paul's preceding comments. In 3:2 he refers to having sent Timothy to "strengthen and encourage" the Thessalonian believers in light of persecution they were experiencing and the risk that they would be "shaken by these persecutions" (3:3). He wants them to be strong so they stand firm in the Lord (3:8). In gratitude to God for the stability already evident in their faith, Paul expresses his prayerful desires that God would allow him to see them again and "restore what is lacking" in their faith (3:10–11), make them "increase and abound in love" (3:12), and strengthen their hearts in holiness with the result of their blamelessness before God when Christ returns (3:13).

31. Arnold, *Ephesians*, 81.

In the context of Paul's preceding remarks, to be strengthened in holiness was to be increasingly secure and confident in God's commitment to them—that God is both faithful and adequate to provide all they need to stand acceptably before God. The recurring motifs of covenant, cleansing from sin, and being in God's presence constitute the active elements of the holiness in which their faith would grow. The term "holiness" in this sense functions as shorthand for all that God has provided in it. Holiness itself does not grow to completion, but growing faith in what holiness provides brings believers to completion.

The apostle Peter made two statements that place holiness in an eschatological light and deserve brief comment.

- **2 Peter 3:11:** "Since all these things are to be dissolved in this way, what sort of persons ought you to be in leading lives of holiness and godliness?"
- **2 Peter 3:14:** "Therefore, beloved, while you are waiting for these things, strive to be found by him at peace, without spot or blemish."

In his second letter, Peter brings "holy" (*hagiais*) and "godly" (*eusebeiais*) together as expectations in light of the eschaton. Verse 14 does not use the *hagios* word group but again draws on the related themes of spotlessness and blamelessness[32] in light of the anticipated new heaven and new earth. These texts do not directly contribute to the profile of accomplished sanctification, but they do reference sanctification/holiness in a punctiliar and holistic sense rather than

32. Andrew M. Mbuvi connects Peter's use of these words to their function in the Old Testament sacrificial system:

> This exhortation to cultic cleanness that makes one worthy of acceptance by God parallels the classification of sacrificial animals as *spotless and without blemish* (Exod 12:5; 29:1; Lev 1:3, 10; Num 6:14). Acceptance before God of the ancient animal sacrifices was premised on this criteria of spotlessness and cleanness, and that remains the same criterion for acceptance of the Petrine community before God. However, while the understanding in the Hebrew Bible was generally a literal application of this phrase to the sacrificial animals, in 2 Peter it becomes a metaphor for spiritual and moral uprightness before God. (*Jude and 2 Peter*, 150 [emphasis original])

a relative or incremental manner. The sanctification given to believers is at the same time an invigorating challenge, compelling them with the prospect of being the type of people who fit in a divinely renewed world.

## Conclusion

The New Testament clearly and unapologetically calls believers toward the pursuit and outworking of sanctified lives. Numerous texts indicate that responding to the call is a process that involves intentionality, seeking God's cleansing from sin, submission to God, and abandonment of competing allegiances. That process leads to increased, and ultimately to full, experiential realization of a cleansed and forgiven heart, awareness of and responsiveness to God's presence, and empowered participation in God's purposes. In this qualified sense, the pursuit and the realization of sanctification are "progressive," though sanctification itself is not progressive.

Scripture offers no clear warrant for the widespread assumption that the actual constituent elements of sanctification somehow increase as if on a graduated scale. Those elements—being claimed by God, being forgiven/cleansed by God, living in God's presence, and being set apart for God's purposes—are decisively given to us by God in sanctification. To each of those elements we are summoned to respond.

Sanctification clearly has direct and powerful implications for our transformation. While Scripture offers no clear case that sanctification itself increases or is synonymous with transformation, what God accomplishes in sanctification provides all that we need for transformation into the image of Jesus Christ. That leads to the specific and practical question: How do we change?

In the next chapter we turn our attention to the linkage between sanctification and transformation, considering texts that commonly figure into sanctification conversations, even though some do not actually talk about sanctification[33] and others speak of it in a rather

33. Acknowledging Michael Allen's point that we cannot assume that a theme (such as sanctification) is not in view simply because it is not mentioned in a biblical

nebulous or unspecified fashion. This linkage reflects the power of what God has already accomplished and continues to accomplish in our sanctification by the Holy Spirit in Jesus Christ. Clarification of this linkage will then free us to pursue transformation out of gratitude and with healthy motivation, but without moralism or narcissistic preoccupation over spiritual self-assessment.

Overall, transformation is about focus. The apostle John promises, "Beloved, we are God's children now; what we will be has not yet been revealed. What we do know is this: when he is revealed, we will be like him, for we will see him as he is. And all who have this hope in him purify themselves, just as he is pure" (1 John 3:2–3). We become what we worship—what captivates our attention.[34]

---

text, we still face the risk of reading inherited theological assumptions about one concept into another concept, resulting in overassociation rather than proper association of those concepts. Although Allen has suggested numerous clarifying nuances about the relationship of sanctification to other biblical themes, it appears that he still assumes greater overlap between sanctification and transformation than the biblical texts will clearly support (*Sanctification*, 28).

34. See J. Smith, *You Are What You Love*. Smith has given popular voice to this theme. His approach to the formational implications of this claim warrants assessment without losing sight of the importance of the claim. I am indebted to my student Chase Davis for his analysis of Smith's approach in his ThM research.

# 7

# Transformation

Serious followers of Jesus Christ long for their impulses, motivations, and habits to reflect the humanity renewed and "regifted" by Jesus. Inevitably, that involves change—transformation from the status quo in that direction. The biblical presentation of transformation clearly depicts something radically different from what we know ourselves to be on our own and apart from Christ. The gap can dishearten, frustrate, even haunt us.

Scripture and experience quickly confirm that we cannot close the gap strictly and simply by our own efforts, regardless of our seriousness and intensity. God must work in us. Discussion and debate continue—sometimes rage—about God's role and our role, and about experiential expectations in the process of becoming "more like Christ." Anyone who acknowledges the primacy of God's role can easily see in Scripture the connection between transformation and sanctification. Sanctification and transformation are clearly related. But how?

Healthy pursuit and experience of transformation depends on accomplished sanctification and on understanding how they are related. The assumption that they are synonymous, or that transformation is synonymous with one aspect of sanctification ("progressive"), seems to create as many problems as it attempts to solve. Much controversy over approaches to transformation, whether categorized as "discipleship" or "spiritual formation," stems from how the relationship between sanctification and transformation is understood.

The consecration profile in the Old Testament begins in covenantal relationship with God. In light of that relationship, God's people were set apart and cleansed for God's purposes, and for being in God's presence. In the New Testament, sanctification is the divinely initiated and divinely animated accomplishment that brings those features into even sharper focus for all believers in Jesus Christ by the work of the Holy Spirit. It is completed on our behalf; not implying that our character or maturity is complete but that we now exist in a particular type of relationship with God that obligates, propels, and resources us for growth into the character of that relationship and into the likeness of the God with whom we relate.

The New Testament evidence does not portray sanctification, per se, as movement or forward progress. Rather, sanctification provides the relationship, resources, expectations, and direction for that movement. Sanctification puts down the markers or rails that guide the growth process, illuminating what transformation is about if it is truly to be Christian transformation and not merely general growth in human virtue.

## Sanctified Transformation

Sanctification points to the nature of maturity in Christ—that toward which we are being transformed. In that light, then, we can read New Testament texts that speak directly of transformation, as well as the sanctification texts that seem to imply transformation or are often associated with transformation.

### *Romans 12:1–2*

> I appeal to you therefore, brothers and sisters, by the mercies of God, to present your bodies as a living sacrifice, holy and acceptable to God, which is your spiritual worship. Do not be conformed to this world, but be transformed by the renewing of your minds, so that you may discern what is the will of God—what is good and acceptable and perfect.

In the previous chapter, we examined the specific role that holiness/sanctification plays in this monumental text. Now it deserves a second look for the illuminating treatment of transformation that makes up part of Paul's multifaceted imperative. C. E. B. Cranfield's description of the transformation that Paul enjoined shows how it depends on what has already occurred so powerfully in the sanctification of the believer. He is worth quoting at length:

> If [Christians] understand what God has done for them in Christ, they know that they belong, by virtue of God's merciful decision, to His new order, and therefore cannot be content to go on allowing themselves to be continually stamped afresh with the stamp of this age that is passing away. On the basis of the gospel, in the light of "the mercies of God," there is only one possibility that is properly open to them, and that is to resist this process of being continually moulded and fashioned according to the pattern of this present age with its conventions and its standards of values. The good news, to which the imperative . . . bears witness, is that they are no longer the helpless victims of tyrannizing forces, but are able to resist this pressure which comes both from without and from within, because God's merciful action in Christ has provided the basis of resistance. In the situation in which he is placed by the gospel the Christian may and must, and—by the enabling of the Holy Spirit—can, resist the pressures to conformity with this age. . . . Instead of going on contentedly and complacently allowing himself to be stamped afresh and moulded by the fashion of this world, he is now to yield himself to a different pressure, to the direction of the Spirit of God. He is to allow himself to be transformed continually, remoulded, remade, so that his life here and now may more and more clearly exhibit signs and tokens of the coming order of God, that order which has already come—in Christ.[1]

The sanctifying presence of God in Jesus Christ and through the Holy Spirit provides the impetus, resources, and focus for this transformation. The familiar indicative–imperative formulation is helpful in summarizing this relationship, but it does not always capture the powerful dynamic at work in the "indicative." In light

1. Cranfield, *Epistle to the Romans*, 2:608.

of "the situation personified in chapter 5 as 'Adam,'" Fleming Rutledge asks,

> How do we escape such captivity? A typical response to this question would be to urge greater religious or moral effort, but that is not the gospel. How then are we to understand the source of transformation? . . .
>
> [Renewal, *anakainōsis*] means *"to become the righteousness of God"*—a transformation that only God can generate—as in II Corinthians 5:21. . . . This is not a process that God begins in us, followed by his stepping aside to observe how we will respond. God is *in* this from first to last, because to be "in Christ" is to be continually made new by the power of the Spirit. . . .
>
> The imperative ["be transformed"] is not only *dependent upon* but *organically produced by* the indicative, or declarative, proclamation: you have died with Christ.[2]

Rutledge's immediate concern is the nature of righteousness (*dikaiosyne*, δικαιοσύνη) as a divine, performative speech act and not merely a descriptive statement as if from a distance. This act grounds transformation in the new reality that God is personally at work. Holiness marks the response of those who have been made righteous and who, rejecting conformity to the world, subject themselves to God's transforming work. Thus, sanctification places believers in the transforming context of God's presence and God's active work. It obligates believers to submit themselves to transformation, determines the character of transformation, and makes transformation possible.

### *2 Corinthians 3:18*

> And all of us, with unveiled faces, seeing the glory of the Lord as though reflected in a mirror, are being transformed into the same image from one degree of glory to another; for this comes from the Lord, the Spirit.

Paul's remarks here did not explicitly equate sanctification and transformation but assume a vital type of linkage between them. He insists that transformation results from the Holy Spirit, whom we know is the divine agent of sanctification. The trajectory of the

2. Rutledge, *Crucifixion*, 557–58 (emphasis original).

transformation process is aimed at increased Christlikeness, as captured in Paul's repeated reference to Jesus as the *imago Dei.* Seeing the Lord's glory plays the instrumental role.

David Garland highlights the Mosaic connection in Paul's imagery: "Paul concludes this section by combining the text of Exodus 34:35 with a commentary. Moses wore the veil over his shining face until he went in to speak with the Lord; and Paul asserts that all Christians can, like Moses, approach the glory of the Lord with unveiled faces and experience the same transformation."[3] Paul's language leaves no doubt that this growth is a process, as Linda Belleville observes, adding that "transformation is not a one-shot affair."[4]

The connections with sanctification become prominent, even inviting and compelling, as we consider how sanctification contributes to transformation. Transformation occurs in and as a result of the Lord's presence—where sanctification places us. George Guthrie expresses this vibrantly:

> Unveiled hearts allow the message to be heard, understood, and responded to. Unveiled faces have open access to God's presence and thus are contemplating the glory of the Lord (4:6) as they are in a constant process of transformation by the Spirit. . . .
>
> As Moses was changed by his encounter with God (Exod. 34:29–30), so those of the new covenant are changed by their experience of the presence of God through the ministry of the Spirit. . . .
>
> Paul is saying that the Christian's transformation by being in the presence of the Lord parallels Moses's transformation by the Spirit. . . . We are made glorious by our observation of the Lord's glory as we experience his presence.[5]

David Garland harmonizes with these observations to create a rapturous score:

> All Christians may approach the Lord as Moses did when he went up Mount Sinai into the presence of the Lord. The results are similar.

3. Garland, *2 Corinthians*, 198. See also Belleville, *2 Corinthians*, 113; Guthrie, *2 Corinthians*, 225.
4. Belleville, *2 Corinthians*, 112.
5. Guthrie, *2 Corinthians*, 227–29.

> Beholding with an unveiled face the glory of the Lord causes us to be transformed into the same image. . . .
>
> We can never encounter God and remain unchanged. Beholding this glory effects our transformation as we are changed into a veritable likeness of him. . . .
>
> It is a moral axiom that we become like the gods we serve (see Rom 1:18–32). In beholding the true glory of the Lord reflected in Christ, our minds become transformed (Rom 12:2) so that we are not conformed to this world and its perceptions and values but conformed to Christ and the paradoxical pattern of his suffering and resurrection (Rom 8:29; Phil 3:10, 21–22). The passive voice, "are being transformed," indicates that this transformation is something done by God, and Paul's exegesis makes clear that it happens through the Spirit.[6]

Craig Keener makes the same point: "In whatever ways this beholding of God's glory is experienced, Paul depicts an ongoing, present experience that brings transformation, just as the same verb for transformation suggests in Romans 12:2."[7] Keener also offers two important reminders. First, "this passage is also relevant in helping us understand Romans 12:2, since 2 Corinthians 3:18 is the only other extant passage where Paul employs the verb μεταμορφόω ('transform')."[8] Second, Paul prefaces his statement in 3:18 with the Holy Spirit's presence and liberating work.[9]

Exposure to the Lord's glory in this way depends on what has been accomplished in sanctification: setting apart, cleansing, and entering the presence of the Lord. We can be and must be transformed because we have been sanctified.[10] From our side of the relationship, the responsibility is to see God as God really is—to be absorbed by God's glory. This fits with Paul's exhortation in Romans 12:1–2 to respond to God's mercy by offering our bodies as sanctified, pleasing sacrifices,[11] not allowing the world to shape us but allowing ourselves

6. Garland, *2 Corinthians*, 199–200.
7. Keener, *Mind of the Spirit*, 215.
8. Keener, *Mind of the Spirit*, 207.
9. Keener, *Mind of the Spirit*, 213.
10. David Peterson helpfully depicts this relationship between sanctification and transformation with two simple graphics. See *Possessed by God*, 37, 77.
11. Lest this sacrifice and the resultant transformation be taken in an overly individualistic way, James Howard draws attention to the ecclesial nature of Paul's

to "be transformed by the renewing of your minds." As our minds are renewed by God, we inevitably experience transformation into what God is like as presented in the person of Jesus Christ.

Worship, then, whatever form it takes, constitutes the foundation, impetus, and power for transformation. In worship we attend and respond to God's presence, which changes us and restores us into God's original intentions. As the degenerating effects of sin can be traced to the withdrawal of humanity from God's presence (Gen. 3), so the culmination of redemption is marked by the unfettered presence of God (Rev. 21–22).[12] Sanctification brings us into the divine presence.

#### *Colossians 3:9–10*

> Do not lie to one another, seeing that you have stripped off the old self with its practices and have clothed yourselves with the new self, which is being renewed in knowledge according to the image of its creator.

Two features of this text add to our understanding of transformation. First, Paul characterizes this glorious renewal in anthropological terms, contrasting the "old" (most likely the fallen, Adamic) self with the "new" self that is distinctly christocentric in orientation.[13] We see anthropological continuity with how God created us and anthropological completion in Christ.

Scot McKnight points out that "the anthropological term 'self' is not primarily individual but especially corporate. This can be argued convincingly if we notice that the so-called new self is the body of Christ, the new community, in verse 11. Hence, the expressions 'old self' and 'new self' are ecclesial: their former life in the world under

---

imperative in Rom. 12:2: "The focus has been shifted from sin and atonement to the service of the believer. . . . The location of the sacrifice has been transferred as well. In the language of the temple cult, the sacrifice of the Old Testament was to be accomplished in the holy place. It is now to be offered up in the true temple of God, the church." Howard also points out that "a sacrifice, by definition, is on behalf of others" (*Paul, the Community, and Progressive Sanctification*, 152–53).

12. I am indebted to Rev. Billy Waters of Wellspring Anglican Church for pointing out the impact of God's presence in the first two and the final two chapters of Scripture, in contrast to everything in between that suffers the degenerating effects of God's presence having been in some sense withdrawn because of sin.

13. Harris, *Colossians and Philemon*, 133.

the principalities and powers and *stoicheia* are contrasted with their new life in the *ekklēsia*."[14] The anthropological character of our renewal points to the body of Christ and our renewal as God's people. This keeps us from thinking about transformation primarily as an individual matter.

Second, this renewal consists of growing knowledge of God. Murray Harris notes, "The unexpressed obj. of the ἐπίγνωσις is God . . . or God's will . . . or both . . . or even Christ."[15]

John Webster ties both of these features to sanctification: "It is perhaps wiser to conceive of the renewal of human nature 'after the image of its creator' (Col. 3.10) in terms which are as broad and as historical as possible: *anakainōsis* [renewal] is the resumption of the history of fellowship between God and his creatures after the vile episode of sin."[16]

#### *1 Thessalonians 5:23*

May the God of peace himself sanctify you entirely; and may your spirit and soul and body be kept sound and blameless at the coming of our Lord Jesus Christ.

As the signature text for John Wesley's theology of entire sanctification, Paul's blessing to the Thessalonians has undergone considerable scrutiny. Without presuming to resolve the points at issue in those well-worn debates (often between the Wesleyan and Reformed traditions), a few comments are in order about how this text fits in the relationship between sanctification and transformation.

Setting aside for the moment the meaning of "entirely"—that is, the extent and nature of the results of God's sanctifying work—what did Paul have in mind about God's sanctifying act itself? Nijay Gupta sees this Pauline prayer/blessing situated in the context of the Thessalonian believers' fear that God had bypassed them (5:1–11) and Paul then offering assurance of God's continued attention to them and work in them (cf. Phil. 1:6). "In keeping with themes

14. McKnight, *Letter to the Colossians*, 311.
15. Harris, *Colossians and Philemon*, 132.
16. Webster, *Holiness*, 85.

found throughout the letter, Paul's focus is on the Thessalonians being formed by God. The divine will is set upon guiding believers towards completeness and maturity in holiness. . . . Paul assures the Thessalonians that this is not an area where believers should be driven by fear [about their insecurities over the future or their own standing before Jesus at his return]. God will see this through, he is both powerful enough and faithful to his promises."[17]

Yet, we must ask: Formation in what sense and how? In light of the Old Testament background to sanctification, which undeniably shaped Paul's thinking about the subject, Paul desired for these believers to experience God's cleansing in every aspect of their lives. Likewise, he wanted them to devote—to consecrate—every dimension of their lives to God for God's service. He hungered for them to live as people who were entirely shaped by the presence of the Living God, for which sanctification had fitted them.

Indeed, there is a process here, but the process is most naturally understood as the continual and expanding submission of their lives to God. Gordon Smith sees being sanctified "through and through" (1 Thess. 5:23 NIV) as referring to the extent of what God has done in believers through union with Christ, which allowed Paul plausibly to call sinners "saints" and which highlights grace as the connecting link between sanctification and justification.

Paul refers to "spirit and soul and body" in typically Hebraic fashion to denote the whole person. The second part of Paul's prayer/blessing, that in the entirety of the persons they would stand before the Lord blameless, fits neatly with the cleansing motif in sanctification and helps qualify what Paul had in mind in the first part of his prayer.[18] As Gupta suggests, Paul envisions God's continual formation of them and their "completeness and maturity in holiness." This formation, completeness, and maturation are the result of what occurs in God's sanctifying work.

To assume that formation, completeness, and maturation are synonymous with sanctification is to read into sanctification what is nowhere found in the biblical lineage of the concept, though the

17. Gupta, *1–2 Thessalonians*, 114–15.
18. G. Smith, *Called to Be Saints*, 50.

entailments of sanctification most definitely effect change in the lives of believers. Paul wanted these believers in Thessalonica to submit their lives—continually, increasingly, in all aspects—to that sanctifying work. That was to mark them until the Lord's return so that the encounter will not be an embarrassment. First Thessalonians 5:23 presents vibrant hope that God will be faithful, based on what he has already done by sanctifying believers, placing them thoroughly and securely in Christ.

#### *Hebrews 10:14*

For by a single offering he has perfected for all time those who are sanctified.

Though Hebrews provides the most direct and concentrated treatment of sanctification as a divinely accomplished reality, this text deserves separate attention because the wording seems to suggest sanctification as a process, especially in conjunction with Romans 6:19 and 2 Corinthians 7:1. What the NRSV translates as "are sanctified" is a present participle (*tous hagiazomenous*, τοὺς ἁγιαζομένους), which can be translated as "are being sanctified," as the ESV does. Do the present tense and middle/passive voice of this verb indicate that sanctification is indeed developmental—a process within believers—in the same sense as transformation?

The immediate and subsequent context, verses 15–18, casts the question back on previous affirmations about sanctification. The Holy Spirit, the writer asserts, reminds them of what their sanctification involved: God's covenant, God's law written on their hearts (Jer. 31:33), and cleansing and forgiveness from sin. Each of these had already taken place for these believers. Thus, "who are sanctified" likely refers to those who are being actively brought by God into the realm of this powerful, life-altering reality.

Another option is presented by Harold Attridge, who sees the participial phrase connoting some type of continual action on the part of individual believers: "The description of the recipients of that perfection as 'those who are being sanctified' (τοὺς ἁγιαζομένους) reinforces the connection between perfection and sanctity that was established in the previous pericope. Yet the present tense used here nuances the relationship, suggesting that the appropriation of the enduring effects of Christ's act is an ongoing present reality."[19] In this sense, what is in process is not sanctification, per se, but believers' reception of, response to, and experiential realization of their holiness.

Some may see this as a merely semantic distinction. However, the significance is in the fact that the constituent features of sanctification—covenantally based setting apart and cleansing, and the presence of God—are not relative or incremental in nature. The quality and consistency of our response to sanctification, however, are indeed relative. They can wax and wane, be better or worse, and grow. What difference does that make? If we confuse our response to sanctification with sanctification itself, then the definitive, propelling, and sustaining work of God that makes us fit for God's presence and God's purposes slips to the periphery of our attention and diminishes in importance as we tacitly presume to take into our own hands the sanctifying work of God that actually factors into our salvation.

The logic of such a move can cripple our spiritual lives. When sanctification is overly associated or improperly associated with the process of transformation, the result is a subtle and insidious version of what the Reformers rejected from the medieval church: justification contingent on or confusedly linked to moral progress. The countermove to avoid that theological landmine is equally hazardous and biblically unsustainable: separating sanctification from God's saving work. The vital course corrective is to situate sanctification properly within the realm of God's saving work, then highlight the transformational resources and implications inherent to it.

Gareth Cockerill grasps this important nuance that sanctification is God's definitive and continual act—continual in the specific sense that God continues to give us these benefits in Christ and we are continually to respond to them. He contends,

> The description of God's people as "those who are being made holy" emphasizes this need for continual participation in the benefits available to Christ's "perfected" and "cleansed" people. The sanctifying

19. Attridge, *Epistle to the Hebrews*, 280–81.

work of Christ is not only definitive (10:10), but continuous (2:10). Thus, the present tense of "being made holy" is not timeless, iterative, or progressive, but simply continuous.

There is nothing in the context that suggests the repeated entering of people into the state of holiness as they are converted. Nor has the pastor been discussing the progress of believers in moral perfection. He is describing the continuous reception of grace from Christ, "the one who makes holy" (2:11). Reception of this grace enables God's people to receive necessary forgiveness and live a life of faithful obedience.[20]

Hebrews 10:14 assumes the accomplished nature of sanctification for such continual action and serves as the basis for the encouraging appeal in 10:19–22 to draw near to God with assurance.

### *2 Peter 1:3–11*

His divine power has given us everything needed for life and godliness, through the knowledge of him who called us by his own glory and goodness. Thus he has given us, through these things, his precious and very great promises, so that through them you may escape from the corruption that is in the world because of lust, and may become participants of the divine nature. For this very reason, you must make every effort to support your faith with goodness, and goodness with knowledge, and knowledge with self-control, and self-control with endurance, and endurance with godliness, and godliness with mutual affection, and mutual affection with love. For if these things are yours and are increasing among you, they keep you from being ineffective and unfruitful in the knowledge of our Lord Jesus Christ. For anyone who lacks these things is nearsighted and blind, and is forgetful of the cleansing of past sins. There, brothers and sisters, be all the more eager to confirm your call and election, for if you do this, you will never stumble. For in this way, entry into the eternal kingdom of our Lord and Savior Jesus Christ will be richly provided for you.

Here Peter utilizes a logic similar to Paul's in Romans 12:1–2, and with the same pastoral integration of concern, invitation, and

20. Cockerill, *Epistle to the Hebrews*, 452.

challenge. Examined closely, Peter's remarks support the case for the dominance of accomplished sanctification. The character imperatives, as well as their progressive nature, stand in response to the clearly accomplished fact that these believers have been cleansed—made holy.

One particular feature of this text warrants attention regarding the relationship between sanctification and transformation. Twice Peter refers to "godliness" (*eusebeia*, εὐσέβεια): first in verse 3 to describe what has been given to us by God's power, and second in verse 6 in the list of character traits that are to increase. Peter also implies a correlation between godliness and holiness in 1 Peter 1:16 when he quotes Leviticus 11:44–45: "Be holy, for I am holy." This connection was crucial for Peter. So in what sense is godliness or holiness to increase?

The various aspects of sanctification—accomplished, imperatival, and eschatological—do not function in a clinically discrete or binary manner. It is not as if any text that appeals primarily to one of those aspects will emphasize only that aspect of sanctification. Peter certainly had some sort of progression in mind, both in the pursuit and in the realization of a godly life. God's power propels the intentional pursuit of godliness and makes possible the fruitful realization of knowing God.

Clearly, Peter cared passionately about growth and transformation. Andrew Mbuvi underscores this emphasis: "Ultimately . . . 2 Peter's concern is with the moral transformation of the community, as verses 5–7 indicate. This would suggest that the form of godliness he has in mind is very closely connected to the community's appropriating of the ethical aspects, which can be rightly described as *godly*, because it is God who empowers them through Jesus, to be able to conform to the virtues listed."[21] Mbuvi also draws attention to the second-person plural construction of the imperatives, concluding that Peter envisions "not individualistic effort but group-oriented drive" and expects these virtues to be "a living reality" in the shared life of this community.[22]

21. Mbuvi, *Jude and 2 Peter*, 76 (emphasis original).
22. Mbuvi, *Jude and 2 Peter*, 78.

After grounding his exhortations in all that God has powerfully done to provide for our godliness, Peter brackets his remarks with both a promise (not "ineffective and unfruitful") and a warning against being "nearsighted and blind" and "forgetful." The reference point for those visual and memory lapses was their cleansing from sins—a central aspect of accomplished sanctification.

Without using the *hagios* word group anywhere in these nine verses (and without referencing every feature involved in it), Peter framed his exhortation for growth on what was accomplished in sanctification. God has acted decisively and powerfully on our behalf: "divine power," "called us," "precious and very great promises" (covenant), "participants of the divine nature" (relational proximity), and "cleansing of past sins."

## Conclusion

The New Testament vigorously insists that the Christian life involves growth and progress, portrayed as transformation into the image of Jesus Christ. Sanctification specifies the christoform content of this transformation. Jesus Christ is the true human, the one fully alive to God with nothing of sin impeding his responsiveness, commitment, and service. Sanctification empowers this transformation, as in it God claims us, places us in the circle of God's covenant commitment, is present to us through the Spirit, and sets us apart for God's purposes in the world. We can and must be transformed because we have been sanctified.

This close and nuanced linkage between accomplished sanctification and transformation shows that the experiential realization of sanctification, which is not identical with sanctification itself, can increase or decrease. Transformation is the fruit of sanctification. To confuse them is to obscure or overlook the powerful work of God that enables transformation in the first place: God's initiative, God's covenant, God's commissioning, and God's presence. This confusion can lead us (functionally, if not formally and consciously) to take on ourselves a type or level of moral responsibility that we cannot fulfill, only to languish under its weight.

When sanctification and transformation are properly related, responsibility and effort do not disappear. Sanctification does not make transformation automatic. Sanctification focuses our attention on the presence and work of God and prompts active, trusting response. In that process, we become like that to which we pay devoted attention in worship.

The journey of transformation is marked by countless variations in personal experience, where much of the debate about sanctification resides. Yet the desire and the expectation for progress in the Christian life are undeniable. As the controlling sanctification motif in Scripture, accomplished sanctification helps us now further explore the theological dimensions of the subject and its practical relationship to transformation.

PART THREE

# The Doctrinal Profile Reanimated

# 8

# Sanctification as God's Transforming Power

If all the "heavy lifting" in sanctification has already been accomplished, does the motivation for obedient, transformative discipleship evaporate? Not at all. Transformation is fueled by the presence of God, where sanctification brings us. Few biblical texts present a more arresting image of this than Isaiah 6:1–8. Isaiah's vision of God—his experience of God's holy presence ("My eyes have seen the King, the LORD of hosts!")—made him excruciatingly and terrifyingly aware of his sin and his need for purification. God provided that purification, then commissioned him for service. Nothing could be more motivating and life-changing, as Peter Gentry points out: "The vision of God given to Isaiah at the beginning of his life and ministry as a prophet profoundly affected his life and radically shaped his message and ministry."[1]

1. Gentry, "The Meaning of 'Holy,'" 409. Gentry also observes, "Isaiah's response confirms the understanding that the basic meaning of holiness is being devoted. Holiness is not identical with moral purity, although there is a connection. Holiness should not be defined as moral purity, but rather purity is the result of being completely devoted to God as defined by the covenant" (413).

Numerous texts that we have examined demonstrate the transformative force of God's presence. Moses's life was forever altered by his encounter with God at the burning bush. God's presence was so powerful that consecration in the Old Testament not only served to allow people to come closer to God but also kept them from coming so close that they would die (Exod. 19)! Sanctification places us in exactly the right, life-giving, and life-altering proximity to God's presence.

Paul reminds the Corinthian church of this in 1 Corinthians 3:16 in order to warn them about the character and conduct of their life together. In 11:28–29 he exhorts them to realize and respect the significance of who they were as Christ's body when they partook of the Lord's Supper. Not to do so, Paul asserts, had actually led to physical illness and death in some cases (11:30). In 14:25 he refers to the fact that God's powerful presence can convict unbelievers when they witness the exercise of the gift of prophecy. There should be no doubt that we are to be deeply affected by acknowledging and responding to God's presence in the specific sense created by sanctification.

The transformation made possible and obligatory by sanctification depends on learning to recognize and respond to the presence of God. The poignant vignettes in which we have seen God's powerfully transformative presence expose something of the unique character of transformation. It is not simple addition of virtue to what is already good about us, what is already in place and in motion in our lives, or the potential that resides in us. No. Present to us in this manner, God judges and exposes, sees straight through us (Heb. 4:13), and dismantles all pretense and falsehood; then God rebuilds and redirects us. T. F. Torrance captured this in his jarring claim that "the grace of God always kills before it makes alive."[2]

In the fall, humanity sought independence from God and as a result lost the presence of God as the animating source of life ("You shall die" [Gen. 2:17]). Accomplished sanctification brings us back into the presence of God, where we can experience the animation

2. I have never found this statement in any of Torrance's published writings, but Ray Anderson recalls Torrance making this statement in his lectures at the University of Edinburgh. See Anderson, *Soul of Ministry*, 47.

and transformation of our lives, flowing out of God's life. Sanctified transformation is entirely grace-oriented because it begins with this divine work of judgment so that genuine life can return, so that life in God can actually occur without illusion or pretense.

Only through attention to what is accomplished in sanctification will transformation not fall prey to the appealing but dead-end illusion of works (transformation as simple addition)—building on what we have in order to make us even better. Improper association of sanctification and transformation unwittingly circumvents proper attention to God's grace-full killing and stripping work in sanctification and moves too hastily to questions of personal responsibility and agency. "Cutting the corner" in this manner anchors our agency (e.g., even through spiritual disciplines) on brittle pylons. It sets us up to experience frustration and to miss the proper work of God in sanctification, which transforms by taking away all human possibility and potential so as then to create in us what we cannot engineer in ourselves—Christlikeness. God's sanctifying power to transform us becomes even more vivid and convincing when we see the personal, divine dynamics at work.

## Accomplished Sanctification as Divine, Dynamic Indicative

We have previously noted the indicative–imperative formulation in reference to how accomplished sanctification relates to sanctification imperatives. As theological shorthand, this formulation captures the primary features of God's defining work vis-à-vis human response and responsibility, and is useful as far as it goes. Yet, as with many theological distillations, it can too easily become clichéd and domesticated, not expressing the full force of *how* the indicative (accomplished sanctification) stands behind and generates the imperatives. This deserves further development in order to show the dynamic force of accomplished sanctification.

This divine indicative represents far more than description of an ontological reality or of the formal authority that exists in a chain of command between God and ourselves (though God's authority is not in question!). In the indicative of accomplished sanctification, God's active, living presence is given. The nature of what is accomplished in sanctification might be compared to active elements that still move around under the earth's crust, creating volcanic activity. As a dynamic activity of God's presence, sanctification has ripple effects. Something has been done that continues to work and unfold. The New Testament writers were so immersed in that reality that they seemed regularly to have this in mind when addressing Christians about the ethical entailments of the gospel.

The indicative–imperative formulation, as such, should be preserved. God's unilateral, objective, comprehensive, and triune work of sanctification (the indicative) precedes human experiential, responsive, ethical obligations (the imperative), both logically and ontologically. The statement still holds true. Yet far more is going on in the indicative than may be evident on the surface, which will influence how we understand and respond to the imperatives. Otherwise, the imperatives suffer from theological malnutrition and quickly take on a moralistic character.

When the indicative of sanctification is seen as an accomplished work of God tightly linked with the believer's union with Christ and identity in Christ, against the backdrop of God's covenantal commitment and powerful presence, the imperatives that flow from it are dynamically supported and animated. This dynamic nature is displayed by the triune character of God's involvement in sanctification.

### *The Christological Character of the Indicative*

The power of this sanctification indicative should create tremors through its christological character. Karl Barth understood as much when he anchored the indicative in the grace of God as given in and through the call of God in Jesus Christ as the Word of God. Barth sought to bypass the dead and deadening implications of identity as merely formal or static, whether in an ontological or conceptual sense.[3]

As shown previously, multiple sanctification texts refer to believers as sanctified "in Christ" (1 Cor. 1:2; Eph. 1:1; Phil. 1:1; Col. 1:2),

3. Barth, *Church Dogmatics*, III/4, 165. See also Deddo, *Karl Barth's Theology of Relations*, 1:75.

which involves both the presence of God and relatedness to God. First Peter 1:22–23 connects the purification involved in holiness with spiritual regeneration through the living Word of God. Newness in Christ (2 Cor. 5:17) and the cleansing through Christ of which sanctification is a part (2 Pet. 1:9) constitute a powerful motivational force for growth. Thus the discipline of remembering God's powerful acts and one's new identity powerfully transforms.[4] This new identity in Christ so constitutes the believer's humanness and the framework for transformation (Col. 3:10) that to live in contradiction to that identity violates something essential.[5] Living at cross-purposes with that identity actually creates dissonance when the believer's personhood has been renewed in union with Christ.[6]

In Romans 6 Paul argues for the believer's death to sin on the basis of the decisiveness of Christ's death and resurrection. Thus he shows how submitting to that work (as slaves to righteousness) in union with Christ (v. 5) leads decisively to the result of sanctification (vv. 19, 22). This is the character and power of accomplished sanctification.

John Murray contends that the death and resurrection of Christ constitute the objective, decisive reality in which those who are elected in Christ died and rose with respect to sin.[7] He points out how Paul shows that Christ's death and resurrection provide the believers' cleansing from sin—an integral feature of sanctification—and break the power of sin.

4. Swiss physician Paul Tournier offered a practical example of this phenomenon: "Nothing can be of greater assistance to a person who feels that life is too much for him than the certainty that God is interested in him personally, and in all he does, that God loves him personally and has confidence in him" (*Adventure of Living*, 113).

5. Grenz, *The Social God*, 240–51. Grenz develops a relational ontology of human personhood based on a version of social trinitarianism.

6. This raises the question of how the *imago Dei* has been affected by sin and, as a result, applies differently, if at all, to those "in Christ" and those apart from Christ. That is, does new identity in Christ imply that the believer's essential personhood is altered in such a way that, by implication, nonbelievers are somehow less in God's image and thus of lesser value as persons? See Kilner, *Dignity and Destiny*. Kilner avoids theological landmines on both sides of this question by focusing on God's intent as the irreducible feature of the *imago Dei*. This theological move locates the ontology of the image outside the human person and upholds human dignity without minimizing the effects of sin on humanity.

7. Murray, "Definitive Sanctification," 12–14.

Being "dead to sin" is not a static, passive state but rather is a defeat of sin's active rule over those in Christ. Thus, being dead to sin means being free and alive to God (the indicative) for the pursuit and realization of holiness (the imperative). Christ's death and resurrection provide cleansing from sin, a new identity of relationship, and liberating power for obedience. Douglas Moo makes this connection: "The Christian is not just called to do right in a vacuum but to do right out of a new and powerful relationship that has already been established."[8] Sanctification is included in the effects of Christ's death and resurrection, along with this new "dead to sin" identity.

In this sense, the purification provided by Christ consistently carries imperatival force (e.g., Acts 15:9; Eph. 5:26; Titus 2:14),[9] which 1 John 3:3 shows as more than merely a moral obligation or logical implication. The imperatival force of purification is expressed through the hope of seeing the Risen and Coming One "as he is" (3:2), which hope is energized by God's love. This new identity—this christological indicative—and the sanctification that it entails are a potent and relational identity, and in this particular manner animate the moral imperatives.

### *The Pneumatological Character of the Indicative*

The Spirit's role in accomplished sanctification must always be understood in connection with what takes place "in Christ." As theologians, theological traditions, and popular literature focus on the Christian life, the Spirit's role in sanctification is generally uncontested. Even so, the focus of the Spirit's sanctifying work is often understood in an instrumental relationship to the process of trans-

8. Moo, *Epistle to the Romans*, 403. Moo goes to great lengths to show the animating character of the indicative–imperative construct that runs throughout Rom. 6. Commenting on verse 2, he argues, "Living a life pleasing to God flows from the real experience of liberation from sin's domain secured by God for us in Christ" (359). He continues, "Paul wants to make clear that 'slavery' [v. 16] is ultimately not just a 'legal' status but a living experience" (398). And, in summary, "Paul makes it clear . . . that we can live a holy life only as we appropriate the benefits of our union with Christ" (391).

9. Murray, "Definitive Sanctification," 6.

formation or is related to accomplished sanctification in primarily an initiating sense, connected to regeneration.

Simply to affirm the Spirit's role in sanctification does not guarantee clarity about how that role functions in sanctification. First Peter 1:1–2 positions the Spirit's sanctifying role as the link between God's election, obedience, and the cleansing provided through Christ. Hebrews 10:29 links the Spirit to God's grace. The sanctifying Spirit of God is the Spirit of the *Living* God, who is every bit as living and active as the Word of God, to whom the Spirit relentlessly bears witness.

Recall Lynn Cohick's insistence that for Paul (in Phil. 3) the Holy Spirit's presence and work constitute the definitive identity of Christians and are thus the basis of holiness.[10] This criterion prompted a radical upgrade in the Jewish church leadership's theology (Acts 15:8) when they recognized gentile believers as full participants in God's grace apart from adherence to Jewish rituals. The gentiles too had been sanctified—made holy—apart from circumcision. This was a radical and staggering prospect for Jews. Imperatives are implicit in this new identity and emerge from this new identity—this Spirit-created indicative that animates the life of Christ in and among those who are in Christ. Through the Spirit, the indicative pulses with the life of God.

Paul's pneumatological appeal for unity in 1 Corinthians 3 stands out in stark relief against the backdrop of the Exodus narrative for what was required of people in general (Exod. 19) and of priests (Exod. 28–29) to approach God's presence. The character of the Corinthians' fellowship was determined by their identity as the temple indwelt by the Holy Spirit, in whose presence they encountered the Living God. The imperatives for their unity were animated by this unique indicative—an indicative created by the presence of the Spirit.

Transformation is to emerge from this new reality and the ethical implications inherent to it. Yet the new reality itself occupies center stage because that reality—that identity—depends on the presence of God. How could being in God's presence and attending/responding

10. Cohick, "We Are the Circumcision."

to that presence not change a person? As the presence of God, the Spirit clarifies the link between sanctification and transformation.

The Spirit is the explicitly stated agent of sanctification. Transformation is a fruit of sanctification. Unless this agency and linkage are made clear, the Spirit's agency in transformation can be seen as overly direct—somewhat automatic or quasi-magical—or bypassed altogether in deference to human responsibility. In either case the Spirit's role is then, perhaps implicitly, placed in tension with human agency, resulting in either passivity or moralism. Thus, the way in which the Spirit's role is understood in the interface between sanctification and transformation provides a theological diagnostic for the perpetual struggle between passivity and moralism.

How is this link between sanctification and transformation activated? In accomplished sanctification the Spirit, as the presence of the Living God, touches and transforms our deepest desires toward God.[11] As James K. A. Smith insists, what we desire changes us.[12] Thankfully, we are not left on our own to generate Godward desires. A Spirit-sanctified vision of God feeds our desire for God and thus changes us specifically toward and into the likeness of Jesus Christ (2 Cor. 4:4; Col. 3:10) as the Spirit exposes us to God's glory through Jesus (2 Cor. 3:18).

David Kelsey compares Paul's emphasis in 2 Corinthians 3:17–18 to the broadly accepted Hellenistic notion of his time that a person could be changed by gazing on deity. "In Paul," Kelsey states, "the connection between 'beholding' the splendor of God and being 'transformed' is located in the context of his understanding of 'faith.'"[13] He continues, "This transformation, which 'comes from the Lord, the Spirit,' is a gift and not an accomplishment."[14]

The sanctifying role of the Spirit differentiates Christian transformation from general growth that is possible for anyone, regardless of religious commitments. Such general (though still meaningful) growth may look every bit as virtuous and have similar social and

11. See Augustine's emphasis on the proper ordering of our loves. Augustine, *On Christian Doctrine* 1.22–35 (pp. 18–30).

12. J. Smith, *You Are What You Love*.

13. Kelsey, *Eccentric Existence*, 2:999.

14. Kelsey, *Eccentric Existence*, 2:1000.

personal benefits, but it falls short of the doxological engagement with God through Jesus Christ where alone is found God's redemptive touch on all aspects of our humanness.

The christological and pneumatological character of the sanctification indicative provides the empowerment for transformation that is uniquely and specifically Christian. When this is overlooked or obscured, the indicative is at risk of being treated in a functionally benign manner and the imperatives are at risk of a functional moralism. The dynamic character of sanctification is thus ignored, and sanctification is understood either negatively, in terms of what not to do, or with a focus on self-improvement, cloaked in theological language. To this day the church struggles against the lingering effects of such understandings of sanctification.

### *The Performative Character of the Indicative*

All that has been said about the christological and pneumatological power of God's sanctifying indicative comes into even sharper focus when this indicative is seen as a divine, performative speech act. As a divine speech act, the indicative created by sanctification in Christ through the Spirit is infinitely more than a description of fact. Scripture is replete with examples of conditions coming into being—things happening—when God speaks.[15]

The performative nature of sanctification as a divine speech act is displayed in John 15:3: "You have already been cleansed by the word that I have spoken to you." The cleansing that Jesus declared was

15. Anthony Thiselton and Kevin Vanhoozer are among those who draw on J. L. Austin's speech-act typology—*locution*, *illocution*, and *perlocution*—to highlight the complex functionalities of biblical revelation as conveyed through human language. See Thiselton, *New Horizons in Hermeneutics*; Vanhoozer, *Drama of Doctrine*; Austin, *How to Do Things with Words*. Though Austin's work has undergone extensive critique and modification by philosophers of language, his basic typology remains useful. See Searle, *Speech Acts*. For another biblical example, Stephen Reid points to the performative character of Ps. 50:7, where God declares, "I am God, your God." Here the divine declaration combines God's self-identification with commitment to the covenant people and constitutes the basis for the injunctions and exhortations that follow. See Reid, "Psalm 50: Prophetic Speech," 227. Reid credits T. Mettinger as "the first to make the connection between Austin's work on performative language and the language of the Psalter" (224).

created by what he had spoken to them on the Father's behalf (see 3:34; 5:47) and served as the basis (the indicative) for his subsequent imperative to "remain" in him (see 15:4).

D. A. Carson comments, "The cleansing power of the word Jesus has spoken to his disciples . . . is equivalent to the life of the vine pulsating through the branches. Jesus' *word* (*logos*) is not assigned magical power. What is meant, rather, is that Jesus' 'teaching' (as *logos* is rendered in 14:23), in its entirety, including what he is and what he does (since he himself is the *logos* incarnate, 1:1, 14), has already taken hold in the life of these followers."[16] Craig Keener attributes this "word" to Jesus's "entire message (14:23–24), which in the context of the Gospel as a whole communicated Christ's very person."[17]

In sanctification as a divine, performative speech act, God actively inaugurates and creates—christologically and pneumatologically—not merely reports. In this sanctifying act God actually brings people into covenant relationship, bestows a purpose on those people, establishes a telos—a future—for them, gives them a new and dynamic identity through God's presence with them, and then compels them forward.[18]

## Accomplished Sanctification, Union, Identity, and Abiding

Finally, the animating, dynamic character of accomplished sanctification is displayed in what it shares with three other New Testament themes: union with Christ, identity in Christ, and abiding in Christ. The christological and pneumatological threadlines shared by these themes suggest that they are not entirely discrete.

These threads show even more of the dynamic theological inner workings in God's sanctifying act: to animate the imperatives, guarantee the future promises, and lead to transformation. Apart from the connections with union, identity, and abiding, accomplished sanctification can be functionally treated as little more than a theological

16. Carson, *Gospel according to John*, 515.

17. Keener, *Gospel of John*, 2:997.

18. Meek, *Loving to Know*, 447. Meek points out that the performative force of divine, covenantal speech acts creates the possibility for us to know God.

"wax figure" that is unable to resource and guide the imperatives and the process of transformation that result from the imperatives.

J. Todd Billings exposes this theological linkage when he calls sanctification "the second dimension of union with Christ" (justification being the first dimension)[19] and observes, "This newly given, legally valid identity leads to the discovery of one's new life in the household of God—a new life of sanctification in which the Spirit calls and empowers Christians to live into their adopted identity."[20] He points out the tight linkage between sanctification and God's saving acts of justification, union, identity, and so forth: "Thus, sanctification is not simply 'our response,' initiated by our asking 'what would Jesus do?' Sanctification, like justification, is a gift that we receive in union with Christ."[21]

John Calvin treats sanctification as the *conditio sine qua non* (indispensable condition) of imperatives to pursue experiential holiness: "Sanctified by Christ's spirit we may cultivate blamelessness and purity of life."[22] In his overall treatment of sanctification, Calvin devotes substantial attention to what has come to be called "progressive sanctification."[23] Sadly, the significance of his emphasis on accomplished sanctification as the basis for all Christian growth has often been eclipsed or underestimated. Other voices in Calvin's legacy also insisted on these connections, yet unfortunately their voices have not continued to receive the attention they deserve.[24]

19. Billings, *Union with Christ*, 13.
20. Billings, *Union with Christ*, 10.
21. Billings, *Union with Christ*, 28.
22. Calvin, *Institutes* 3.11.1.
23. What has come to be seen as Calvin's doctrine of progressive sanctification rests on various statements he made regarding progress in overcoming the effects of indwelling sin, such as, "No one shall set out so inauspiciously as not daily to make some headway, though it be slight. Therefore, let us not cease so to act that we may make some unceasing progress in the way of the Lord" (*Institutes* 3.6.5). Interestingly, Calvin recognized, more than may often be acknowledged, the power involved in the cleansing work of God that precedes the believer's conscious pursuit of godly living through mortification and vivification. He states, "It would not be enough duly to discharge such duties unless the mind itself and the heart first put on the inclination to righteousness, judgment, and mercy. That comes to pass when the Spirit of God so imbues our souls, steeped in his holiness, with both new thoughts and feelings, that they can be rightly considered new" (*Institutes* 3.3.8).
24. See John Owen, "Of the Mortification of Sin in Believers," in *The Works of John Owen*, 6:19. Owen provides one such example through his repeated insistence

## Conclusion

Accomplished sanctification is a dynamic, life-altering, empowering work of God because in it God works personally and immediately through the Son and the Spirit. In these ways, God's presence is never static, never benign, but always active and performative. In one way or another, everything changes in God's presence.

The sanctification themes traced thus far through Scripture find full expression in the New Testament through the saving work of Christ and the resulting combination of believers' union with Christ, new identity in Christ, and abiding in Christ. The presence of God to those in Christ and the consequent empowering of believers for service are brought about by the Holy Spirit. Accomplished sanctification encapsulates everything that occurs to pull forward the Old Testament thread of consecration into the daily lives of all who are in Christ through the Holy Spirit. This proximity to God brings with it a priestly empowerment and the resources for transformation into the image of Christ, who is "God with us."

The overlap among the theological themes explored in this chapter shows that they share an animating core of divine presence and activity. Therein rests all hope and all resources for growth and transformation in Christ. In light of these powerful, animating divine realities we can now examine more closely the process of transformation that garners so much attention in treatments of sanctification.

---

that the "mortification of sin" depends on the Holy Spirit and the resources of Christ given by the Spirit. In the first three chapters of Owen's classic work he lays a thoroughly christological and pneumatological foundation for the mortification of sin. The attention that he devotes to the practices and challenges of mortification in the balance of the work seems to have drawn more attention than this living theological root system. It's reasonable to suspect that the theological nuances and balance of his argument have not garnered nearly as much attention as has his treatment of the disciplines and difficulties of mortification. Unfortunately, then, Owen's work has sometimes been perceived as promoting a moralistic, austere, duty-driven approach to the Christian life.

# 9

# Sanctification and the Process of Transformation

How we understand the relationship between sanctification and transformation makes an enormous difference in how we engage and experience both of them. Whether or not we are conscious of it, our theology of sanctification is at work in how we pursue transformation and wields powerful influence over our Christian experience.

How does sanctification allow and empower transformation? What is our responsibility, our role, in experiencing personal transformation? It is to focus our hearts attentively, habitually, and responsively on the God who has initiated covenant with us, cleansed us from our sins, brought us into God's intimate presence, and set us apart for God's glorious, redemptive purposes in the world. Our responsibility is entirely responsive, though no less intentional and active.

To paraphrase Ecclesiastes 12:12, of making spiritual growth resources and disciplines there is no end. Out of weariness and jadedness, some have resigned themselves to versions of spiritual passivity, often in the name of faith as the direct means of transformation. Admittedly, Romans 12:2 places transformation in the passive voice—"be transformed"—signaling it as the work of God. Yet God's work in transformation, anchored in and propelled by sanctification, does not cancel human responsibility and effort. Texts such as 2 Peter 1:3–11 and Philippians 2:12–13 make this quite clear. Yet, where and how is that intentionality to be focused? All that we have examined about the predominantly accomplished nature of sanctification provides clues and orients our direction. In every instance, human effort is intentional response to divine initiative.

## Response to God's Word

The written Word comes to us as God's most comprehensive means of transformation, always calling forth response. In 2 Timothy 3:16–17 Paul connects Scripture's divine origins ("God-breathed," *theopneustos*) with its divine purpose: that we may be "proficient, equipped for every good work" through the process of "teaching . . . reproof . . . correction, and . . . training in righteousness." God's written Word is a divine change agent because the very breath of God sends it forth and uses it to those ends.

Isaiah 55:10–11 provides a salient example of the inherent power of God's speech acts. To illustrate that power, God uses the example of precipitation that irrigates the earth and causes plants to grow, with the immediate effect of providing bread to eat and the long-term effect of providing more seed to sow. Likewise, God says that the Word "shall not return to me empty, but it shall accomplish that which I purpose and succeed in the thing for which I sent it." All that God has provided through the written Word finds its power in the triune God through the Spirit and the incarnate Word. Nothing has been the same since God spoke into the world through the Son—the *Logos* (John 1:1–14; Heb. 1:1–2; 4:12–13; Rev. 1:16).

The power of the written Word of God is thus not the power of incantations or "magic" words[1] but the power of God's presence, provided for us through sanctification. Although God's written Word does not transform us automatically or instantaneously, through that Word God's presence inherently calls for response, defines the shape or character of that response, and provides the resources for that

1. It is not uncommon, at least at a popular level, for Scripture's power to be understood in this sense.

response (Acts 20:32). Spiritual transformation—genuinely Christian transformation—always involves the Word of God in its trinitarian character, which expands and deepens our mode of engagement with the written Word and our response to it.[2]

## Response to Suffering

Paul identifies suffering as a catalyst for change: "Suffering produces endurance, and endurance produces character, and character produces hope" (Rom. 5:3–4). Anyone who has suffered or observed others who suffer knows that suffering does not have a uniformly or predictably positive effect. Some become bitter and cynical, moving further from God. How and why, then, is suffering a factor in positive spiritual transformation?

Philippians 3:10–12 provides Paul's autobiographical reflection on suffering as his occasion to experience the power of Christ's resurrection in his life. In his case, suffering exposed the uselessness of all other benefits and advantages in his life, compared to the value of knowing Christ. Suffering exposed and stripped him of any illusions about where true life was to be found, setting in relief the "surpassing value" (3:8) of personally knowing Christ. He knew that such life-giving knowledge of God was possible only through the type and extent of divine power exercised in a literal resurrection. What happened in Paul's sanctification allowed suffering to have this transformative effect on him.

In Romans 5 he places hope as an end product of suffering and promises that "hope does not disappoint us, because God's love has been poured into our hearts through the Holy Spirit that has been given to us" (v. 5). Here we see the effect of the divine presence given in sanctification. God's love becomes real and transforming through the Holy Spirit. God's love is so real as to evoke hope that ameliorates

2. There is far more to be said about this. The evangelical priority on the formative power of Scripture in discipleship is an enormous asset. Yet, the role of Scripture in discipleship and spiritual formation needs more of the type of attention that it has happily received in, for example, E. Howard, *Guide to Christian Spiritual Formation*; Mulholland, *Shaped by the Word*.

and transcends whatever messages of discouragement and futility suffering may send our way. One of the dynamic, transformative implications of accomplished sanctification is that God's power actually operates in our lives to uphold and focus our lives with hope in the midst of suffering. Only the presence of God through the Holy Spirit, given through God's sanctifying work, can have such remarkable effects.

God's Word and suffering are but two means by which God transforms us. In each case transformation occurs as a result of our response to divine presence and power given to us through sanctification by the Holy Spirit. Perhaps not as familiar, however, is how the transformative effects of accomplished sanctification occur in worship.

## Response in Worship

Worship, especially corporate worship, is a relatively recent topic of discussion and research within some sectors of evangelicalism.[3] For many Christians worship has long been valued as an occasion to learn and to offer to God gratitude, praise, and prayer. Yet within this framework the formative role of worship has generally been understood in terms of what happens as a result of preaching and teaching sessions.

The transformative power of worship comes into view when we consider the corporate as well as individual nature of God's indwelling, transforming presence. When we consider the church as God's dwelling place in light of tabernacle and temple imagery, the connections to sanctification are almost impossible to miss.

Corporate liturgical expressions (whether formal or informal, "high" or "low," liturgies) and "life together"[4] are foundational for personal efforts in transformation.[5] In such corporate response to God's covenantal work of redemption, believers abide in God's pres-

3. Recall the flurry of interest created by a spate of evangelical publications on the subject of worship in the early 1980s—for example, Allen and Borror, *Worship*. See also Martin, *Worship of God*.

4. See Bonhoeffer, *Life Together*.

5. See again James Howard's presentation of the Pauline case on this point in *Paul, the Community, and Progressive Sanctification*.

ence in a specific manner. This in no way minimizes the omnipresence of God or reverts to a medieval sacred-secular dualism. It simply acknowledges that God chooses to be present to people and interact with them in particular ways in their corporate life and worship.

T. F. Torrance locates the transformative character of the church's worship in its sanctification: "The Israel of the Old Testament was a holy people *because God hallowed or sanctified himself in its midst*. By bestowing upon it his own presence he brought it within the sphere of his own holiness. Thus the very term 'holy' carries with it the notion of the church as the sphere among humanity of God's hallowing."[6] Luke's bracing account of Ananias and Sapphira in Acts 5:1–11 demonstrates without any doubt the transformative effects of God's presence among God's people, even in the gift-giving aspect of their corporate life. The conclusion of the narrative in verse 11 puts it bluntly: "Great fear seized the whole church and all who heard of these things." God's presence to the gathered church changes people.

The writer to the Hebrews offered a complementary ecclesial example (Heb. 10:19–25), inviting believers into God's presence with assurance because of the cleansing that they have been given through Christ's sacrifice. The writer then calls them to lives of hope and constant, mutual encouragement. To be encouraged changes our course in deeply practical ways. We make different decisions, take different paths, and are actually different as a result of encouragement.

We must not see only the imperatives in these texts. Every bit as prominent are the transformative imprints of response to those imperatives. To live with such love, gratitude, and mutual commitment, and to do so in direct response to God through Jesus Christ, can come about only because of the work that God does for us in sanctification: choosing and calling, cleansing, bringing into God's presence, and setting apart for service.

The biblical narrative is dramatically laced with the insistence that we become like what we worship. Psalm 115:4–8 and 135:15–18 depict those who worship handmade idols as being diminished to the mute and deaf status of the objects they trust. "Those who make

6. Torrance, *Atonement*, 385 (emphasis original).

them and all who trust them shall become like them" (135:18). The trusting, worshiping focus of our hearts will transform us, one way or another.

Hebrews 12 challenges God's sanctified people to diligence and intentionality, assuring us of what God has accomplished for us decisively through Christ, and reminding us to look "to Jesus the pioneer and perfecter of our faith" (v. 2). This assurance, along with perspective on the Lord's discipline of the beloved (vv. 5–11), grounds the call to pursue holiness (v. 14) and aims that pursuit at the full, experiential realization of what has already been given to us in Jesus our forerunner. Intentional effort, framed by God's loving discipline of our lives, is no less diligent and no more legalistic for being entirely responsive in nature. The intense, faith-oriented focus of our lives on what God has gracefully accomplished for us in sanctification leads to transformation for which we can only offer gratitude.

## Response in Gratitude

Whatever we ultimately trust compels the focus of our lives. What we trust shapes us profoundly. What we trust is what we look to for our deepest sustenance and what will inevitably be the focus of our gratitude. Our gratitude, then, is an indicator of what we trust and can be a discipline for the transforming focus of our lives. The transformative character of gratitude shows up particularly in the context of ecclesial worship as we submit ourselves to liturgical disciplines of giving thanks to God and interact with others whose gratitude pulls us through our seasons of personal ingratitude.

Gordon Smith describes how the discipline of gratitude increases our capacities for living in the love of God—that is, living out of our union with Christ.[7] Gratitude can be easily overlooked or trivialized as an expression of good manners and socialization in healthy relationships but otherwise not deeply life-altering. Yet in Romans 1:18–23 Paul placed lack of gratitude to God (v. 21) alongside un-

7. G. Smith, *Called to Be Saints*, 171–74.

godliness, wickedness, suppression of the truth, and idolatry—all descriptions of those who do not give glory to God and who stand under God's wrath without excuse.

Gratitude, then, mirrors the posture of our hearts toward God and serves either to close or open our hearts to God. Gratitude is integral to worship (e.g., 1 Cor. 10:16; 14:16). Richard Lints links worship and sanctification in this manner, stating, "In sanctification it is not a believer's moral progress in view, but rather the (relative) restoration of their worship organs."[8] Sanctification effects this doxological restoration, which then makes possible everything that the Scriptures call transformation.

The discipline of remembering figures into this grateful responsiveness. Peter's straightforward exhortations to intentional cultivation of growth (2 Pet. 1:3–11) are rooted in vision and memory of God's power (v. 3), God's promises (v. 4), and God's cleansing us of our sin (v. 9). Our efforts toward transformation and growth include intentional acts of memory—not merely calling to mind certain claims but also reentering and resubmitting ourselves to those realities. This type of remembering was to undergird the faithfulness of God's covenant people in the Old Testament (Num. 15:39–40; Deut. 8:2, 11, 18–19; Josh. 4:7) and continues through the New Testament as a powerfully formative act (Eph. 2:11–12; Rev. 3:3).

The modern, Western tendency toward compartmentalization of our rational faculties allows the act of remembering to be domesticated as a benign mental exercise. Yet, Scripture presents remembering as powerfully influential in the life of faith.[9] The discipline

8. Lints, "Living by Faith—Alone?," 55.

9. Sifers, "The Armor of God," 83–97. Sifers argues that Paul's imperative to "put on the full armor of God" in Eph. 6:11 functions as a multilayered metaphor by which Paul appeals to his readers thus to reengage something that has already happened, rather than literally to put something "on" that otherwise is "off." To reimagine ourselves in that armor provides strength to "stand against the devil's schemes." Cognitive scientist Benjamin K. Bergen uses the phrase "embodied simulation" to depict mental visualization (simulation) that "makes use of the same parts of the brain that are dedicated to directly interacting with the world. When we simulate seeing, we use the parts of the brain that allow us to see the world; when we simulate performing actions, the parts of the brain that direct physical action light up" (*Louder Than Words*, 14–15).

of remembering what God has done and who we are as sanctified ones constitutes a powerfully formative act of continual, personal reengagement.

In this sense accomplished sanctification protects against moralism as we strive to grow in Christ. John Webster clarifies this point: "Tying sanctifying so firmly to divine agency enters a protest against exemplarist accounts of the atonement in which the work of Christ is reduced to the mere occasion, stimulus or pattern for the Christian's efforts to become holy through works of holiness. . . . As mortification, holiness is the laying aside of that which has been put to death at the cross of the Son of God; as vivification, holiness is the living out of that which has been made alive in the Son's resurrection."[10]

Disciplined, deliberate, cultivated gratitude cuts through the tension between grace, faith, and effort. Discipline then becomes trusting response to God's gracious presence and gracious saving/sanctifying work for us. All discipline is no less energetic and intentional as it moves forward in the freedom of gratitude.

Spiritual discipline for transformation habituates responses that reflect the character of holiness. Only as our focus is so habituated or continuously calibrated by sanctification will intentional engagement, effort, and change be animated by grace. Only thus will our efforts avoid debilitating and spiritually toxic moralism that results from isolated emphasis on the imperatives of sanctification rather than on what is powerfully accomplished through sanctification. To "pursue holiness" is not to acquire something external to us, but rather to let ourselves be shaped by our new relational reality in Christ.[11] This new identity in Christ and in union with Christ is created and sustained by the Spirit, who works out Christ's life in us.

10. Webster, *Holiness*, 81, 88.

11. It is noteworthy here that one of the meanings of the Greek verb *diōkō* (διώκω), most often translated as "pursue," as in Heb. 12:14, is "practice." Compare the use of *diōkō* in Rom. 12:13 (NIV: "practice hospitality"). See also its use in 1 Cor. 14:1, which in the J. B. Phillips Version is translated as "Follow, then, in the way of love." Thus, "pursue holiness" perhaps could be understood to mean "practice holiness" or "follow in the way that holiness leads."

## Conclusion

Though some New Testament epistles end on a hortatory note, they still embody the dominant power of God's decisive work and promises. At the end of Romans, after having made such a forthright call for transformation, Paul affirms God's work in those believers: "I myself feel confident about you, my brothers and sisters, that you yourselves are full of goodness, filled with all knowledge, and able to instruct one another" (15:14).

This chapter has explored our role in the process of transformation as it is rooted in sanctification. God's presence, made available through sanctification, constitutes the primary catalyst for transformation. Instrumentally, God transforms us through the Word, our suffering, and corporate life and worship, as with each of these we cultivate habits of grateful, Godward responsiveness, made possible only through God's sanctifying work.

Nothing God has done to sanctify us replaces or precludes our intentional, personal engagement. The Spirit's role in sanctification and transformation does not allow for passivity. Rather, the Spirit's role in sanctification constitutes all pursuit and realization of personal growth in godly character as a gift rather than an accomplishment. When sanctification is confused with transformation and when sanctification is thus portrayed as primarily out in front of us rather than accomplished for us, sanctification quickly takes on moralistic tones, veers in an overly anthropocentric direction, and can foster spiritual narcissism.

Having been sanctified by the Spirit in Jesus Christ, we can and must allow that holiness to take over and be reflected in every area of our lives. All that is accomplished in sanctification places within the scope of God's grace our responsibility to do what is necessary for transformation to occur. Thus, we can make use of every resource to bring our lives into conformity with God's intentions for human personhood.

# 10

# Accomplished Sanctification in Action

If the accomplished aspect of sanctification dominates and defines the doctrine of sanctification, the difference will be evident in life and not merely on paper. Therefore, our study will conclude with a few examples of how accomplished sanctification can affect our lives. These are merely suggestive and offered in hopes of fostering generative discussions of what accomplished sanctification can provide for spiritual transformation.

God's decisive and dynamic action in sanctification sets the pace for our pursuit of transformation and for the sanctification promises that await us. The implications are substantial and liberating. What God has accomplished in sanctification is therapeutic in its relational implications. We belong. We are seen and known as we are, and still claimed and given purpose even though the quality of our lives does not match the glory and truth of the mission we have been given. Through sanctification we are commissioned to be agents of blessing in Jesus's name, in whatever setting and role and circumstances we find ourselves.

Each aspect of transformation still calls for something conscious and intentional from us. For far too long, disproportioned portrayals of sanctification have fed unnecessary polarities in the field of discipleship and spiritual formation. A biblically proportioned understanding of sanctification goes far toward alleviating that tension.

## No Polarization of Grace and Effort

As mentioned above, grace and faith are commonly placed in tension with effort. Some movements attempt to resolve this tension by opting for grace and faith over effort.[1] Others posit an asymmetrical relationship between monergism in justification and synergism in sanctification,[2] which assumes a type of distinction between justification and sanctification that the biblical evidence does not clearly support.[3]

Accomplished sanctification opens a path through these tensions by validating the mysterious interface between God's accomplished work and our responsibility. In other words, we need not provide an analytical schematic for the interface between grace, faith, and human responsibility/effort, as if transformative energy were a fixed commodity that must be managed with just the right algorithm.

The interface between the Spirit's work in sanctification and transformation defies reduction to specific formulas. While God can and

1. This has been a hallmark of the Keswick tradition. See also Thrall, McNicol, and Lynch, *Truefaced*, 99–100. Thrall, McNicol, and Lynch argue for a faith-driven appropriation of our new identity in Christ that is quite similar to the way accomplished sanctification influences and leads to transformation. In making this case, they offer a more nuanced view of the relationship between grace/faith and effort, delineating two types or directions of effort—what they call "two rooms." One type strives to please God and the other responds to the fact that God is already pleased. However, they periodically make statements that subtly blur sanctification and transformation in a manner that goes beyond mere semantic confusion, both reflecting and fostering the type of practical problem addressed earlier in this work. For example, "God is not interested in changing the Christian. He already has." For an example of attempts to relate grace/faith and effort properly, note Dallas Willard's often-quoted maxim: "Grace is not opposed to effort, it is opposed to earning. Earning is an attitude. Effort is an action" (*Great Omission*, 61).

2. This way of framing the relationship has marked the Reformed tradition and is exemplified in the writings of J. I. Packer.

3. Peterson, *Possessed by God*, 43–44.

occasionally does intervene more directly and immediately in personal transformation, such interventions are no more to be expected as a predictable pattern than are other miraculous interventions in the created order.

God's sanctifying work also eliminates the tension between transformation, when perceived as God's unique work of grace for believers, and the change available to anyone, regardless of their faith commitment. Research and discoveries in the area of neurobiology and neuroplasticity provide one of the most recent and challenging examples of this dilemma.

Neuroscience research has shown that people possess inherent and remarkable capacities for growth and change, far exceeding what was long believed possible[4] because of determinism or theological appeals to depravity. Previously unimaginable capacity for personal change is accessible by knowing how the human brain functions and how to restructure its neuropathways. A sanctification-based theology of transformation is unthreatened and actually strengthened by these discoveries when the true nature of biblical transformation is clarified through the lens of the sanctification that undergirds it.

Changes in structural capacities and habits occur for Christians—those sanctified by the Spirit—within the same biological structures as they do for others, hence the value of neuroplasticity and other resources by which any person is able to change seemingly intractable features of their lives. Personal transformation of the type envisioned and enjoined in Scripture may involve more than what neurological structures can account for, but such transformation does not necessarily involve less. Craig Keener acknowledges this reality and places it in theological perspective:

> Unfortunately, our negative choices also wire our brains for particular neurochemical responses, so that we become accustomed to respond to stimuli in such detrimental ways automatically. In such cases, walking by the Spirit rather than by the flesh requires a continuing, deliberate rethinking and retuning, with many determined decisions

4. For the popular and practical implications of these developments in neuroscience, see Duhigg, *The Power of Habit*; Patterson et al., *Change Anything*.

> to believe God's truth about our identity, until our brain is rewired enough that the new way becomes the more prevalent way. Even so, the old memories and patterns may resurface, especially under stress, whether in dreams or while awake, and therefore continued vigilance is important.[5]

Though the Spirit is free, as God, to work in even the most dramatic and uncanny ways, the distinct work of the Spirit is not a substitute mechanism for what we know about the biological structures in which human change is grounded. Rather, the Spirit's unique activity is the orientation and constant reorientation of our focus and affections to Jesus Christ, which does not and cannot happen without the Spirit.

Thus, by clarifying the nature of transformation as growth in Christlikeness, the accomplished nature of sanctification provides grace to endure the frustrations of striving and trusting God when there is little apparent or sustainable change. And it helps alleviate confusion about the phenomenon of those who experience significant growth and life change apart from Christian faith.

## Flexible Models of Spiritual Growth

Scripture presents no single model for the pursuit and experience of growth in Christlikeness. Various models, or features of them, speak meaningfully into the complex variables of individual spiritual journeys. These models need not be polarized, as is so often the case. What God accomplishes for our sanctification expands the terrain for models of spiritual growth.

The Christian life involves struggle, though the content and experience of that struggle may vary from issue to issue and from person to person. There must be surrender—relentless faith in God through Christ and by the Spirit—though the specific focal point of that trusting surrender may differ from one challenge to another. There are

5. Keener, *Mind of the Spirit*, 263. Even the resources of neuroscience cannot alter our core desires in the direction of Christlikeness or fashion our efforts toward that end.

always common features of this faith: trust in God's adequacy and provision, in God's goodness and sovereign purposes, and so forth. Sometimes such trust results in a restful peace and a sense of release. At other times this trust provides the impetus and confidence for vigorous struggle.

Discipline is always demanded, though the notion of spiritual discipline is sometimes saddled with moralistic baggage from environments that were manipulative, disheartening, and even abusive. Sadly, this has poisoned the notion of discipline for many believers who sincerely want to grow in Christlikeness. Yet it is impossible to defend from Scripture any notion of growth in Christlikeness apart from disciplined cultivation of Christlike character and habits of responsiveness to God and others. In accomplished sanctification God is gracefully present to foster healthy spiritual discipline and protect it from toxicities that would pit it against God's grace.

The process of growth in Christ, with all its mystery and vicissitudes, is undergirded and guaranteed by God, who "began a good work" and "will bring it to completion by the day of Jesus Christ" (Phil. 1:6). Indeed, only a few sentences prior to that assurance, Paul addresses the Philippian believers as the "saints"—that is, the holy ones, the sanctified ones. Then he brackets those assuring words with exhortations to "live your life in a manner worthy of the gospel of Christ" (1:27) and "work out your own salvation with fear and trembling; for it is God who is at work in you, enabling you both to will and to work for his good pleasure" (2:12–13). All motivation and discipline that the doctrine of sanctification incites in us can be sustained by this assurance.

The fact that our sanctification has been accomplished will create a sense of conviction of sin at times, and lead to repentance. It will involve a healthy sense of guilt at times. Yet any motivation created thereby is not aimed at getting sanctification back or getting more of it. The impetus for repentance and the motivation to pursue Christ stem from the reminder that we have already been claimed, called, cleansed, brought into God's presence, and given a divine mission. Getting back on track or trying to stay on track and move forward is possible and conceivable only because we have been sanctified in Jesus Christ by the Holy Spirit.

**Transformed Assessment**

Through accomplished sanctification, transformation is not bound to linear, measurable, cumulative experiences of growth. Frustration and ongoing struggle (as long as it actually is struggle, not mere acquiescence in the name of struggle) do not invalidate sanctification, transformation, or newness in a believer's life. Frustration and struggle can actually indicate the mysterious nature of the Spirit's empowering presence (John 3:5–8).[6] Any model of the Christian life that attempts to codify or standardize the Spirit's role will inevitably miss something and frustrate the process for those with whom the Spirit interacts in the Spirit's hidden manner.

God's accomplished act of sanctification alleviates the burdensome assumption that transformation is only linear, cumulative progress. Growth often occurs in the complex intersections of sin, grace, and struggle. Some struggles accompany us all of our lives. Thus, growth does not necessarily consist of overcoming or eliminating struggles but of habitually leaning more faithfully into God's grace for those struggles. Paul knew exactly this after he prayed three times for God to remove an unnamed affliction, only to receive assurance that God's grace was sufficient for him (2 Cor. 12:7–9). Presumably, the purpose of God's grace in his case was that Paul would deal with the affliction faithfully. However much we might resist the notion, even ongoing struggles are sanctified occasions to recognize and respond to God's presence in them.

As Donald Bloesch observes, "One can turn one's failures and defeats into redemptive cross-bearing by offering them up to God to be used to enlighten and benefit others who are going through similar struggles."[7] He also notes, "The Christian faith affirms not that everything in the world is holy but that anything might become holy under the impact of the Spirit."[8] Sanctified struggles do not necessarily disappear, as enticing as that notion is. Rather, those struggles become holy as the fulfillment of God's missional purposes

6. Kelsey, *Eccentric Existence*, 1:443. See Kelsey's description of the "circumambient" nature of the Spirit's work.

7. Bloesch, *Theological Notebook*, 1:47.

8. Bloesch, *Theological Notebook*, 2:17.

in our lives. Accomplished sanctification assures us that not only ordinary "places" but even the broken places in our lives are encompassed in our sanctification as God becomes present to us in those places, interacts with us there, and makes those places useful for God's purposes.

This sense that an ongoing, intense struggle can be sanctified may feel counterintuitive because inner conflict seems so incompatible with the pleasure and presence of God. Yet what could be more pleasing to God than our trust that God's presence with us is more real and definitive than our struggles? What could be more holy than the fact that God is pleased to be at our side as our advocate when we struggle? The transformation that emerges from sanctification provides freedom to bring our struggles and brokenness into God's presence for God to redeem or reframe or defuse them, rather than to feel caught between our struggles and God, with God as our adversary rather than as our advocate. Accomplished sanctification, and awareness of it, provides what we need to move forward into the risks and demands of obedience, knowing that God is with us and for us.

Accomplished sanctification sharpens our understanding of what counts as growth and transformation. Sanctified transformation brings healing and expansion of our fallen and damaged capacities for faith, hope, and love. This transformation habituates our defaults to seek and receive forgiveness, to return to God, to have faith to serve again. It allows us to see growth as grateful responsiveness to God and dependence on God, regardless of whether we can track cumulative progress or the diminishment of struggles.

Biblical ethical imperatives can be accepted for what they are without the assumption that they imply self-justification before God. They need not be mistaken for moralistic attempts to please God in ways that Christ has already done on our behalf. Instead, these imperatives can be accepted and followed as the voice of the One who has claimed us, brought us into intimacy, and given us all that we need to live and serve well. The imperatives rest on who we have been made to be.

We may do all of this well or poorly or both, at different periods and in different areas of life. We may realize encouraging, progressive gains in some areas of life and recycled struggles or setbacks in others. None of those phenomena reflect on our sanctification.

Transformation into the image of Christ depends on what God has accomplished in sanctification. Yet, our sanctification is not in question if our transformation is spotty and inconsistent.

## Conclusion

In light of its Old Testament roots, New Testament development, and theological connections, accomplished sanctification offers the dynamic commitment, presence, and power of God to graciously animate and transform our lives. We have merely touched on a few frequently confusing or conflicted areas of the Christian life: the relationship of God's grace to our efforts and resources, the models by which we interpret and engage the process of spiritual transformation, the criteria by which we assess our growth in Christian maturity, and the question of how God's purposes are fulfilled through the checkered nature of our daily experience.

Fruitful exploration of any of these and related questions depends in part on our framework of assumptions about sanctification. A refreshed biblical and theological understanding of the accomplished aspect of sanctification provides the resources we need in order to make meaningful progress as we engage those questions. Accomplished sanctification is not the sum total of what Scripture teaches about sanctification, but it controls the conversation in ways that have long been overlooked, to our detriment. It breathes the breath of God into otherwise dead and dusty places.

# Conclusion

This study has ranged across history, Scripture, and theology to suggest a reproportioning of the doctrine of sanctification. Though each of these domains could be explored in much greater depth, each area offers sufficient evidence to prompt a second look at long-standing assumptions about sanctification, regardless of one's Christian tradition and personal discipleship history.

In these domains of study we have examined challenges presented by the doctrine of sanctification, some history of the doctrine's development, the assertions made by key biblical passages, and how those assertions work together. Four primary assumptions have undergirded this study. First, there is an implicit logic or profile to how the different aspects of the doctrine of sanctification fit and function together. That composite profile tells a particular story about what it means for God's people to be sanctified.

Second, when we emphasize the doctrine of sanctification in ways that reflect that profile, sanctification is empowering, compelling, and life-giving, as well as challenging and indicting. To the extent that our emphases on sanctification are imbalanced, distorted, or otherwise inconsistent with that profile, the doctrine can actually impede what the biblical writers envisioned.

Third, the accomplished aspect of sanctification sets the pace or establishes the framework for everything else Scripture says about the subject. Every other aspect of the sanctification profile—especially imperatives and references to sanctification as yet to be completed—is determined by what happens in accomplished sanctification and must be interpreted in that light.

Fourth, sanctification and transformation are not synonymous but are linked. Transformation depends on sanctification. Theological traditions that overly associate sanctification with transformation can either tacitly burden believers more than help them flourish or foster spiritual apathy and presumption. The former prioritizes human responsibility and synergism in sanctification. Yet, intentional effort can become burdensome and disheartening when not properly nourished by God's gracious actions expressed in sanctification. The latter assumes that transformation either occurs instantaneously or takes care of itself as long as one properly rests in one's sanctification. Disciplined effort to grow in Christlikeness is therefore suspect by association with legalism, and sanctification imperatives are easily ignored or explained away.[1]

A reproportioning and refreshment of the doctrine of sanctification demands three tasks in light of how the doctrine takes shape throughout the canon of Holy Scripture. First, some of the language commonly used when talking about sanctification needs to undergo a "scrubbing" so that our doctrinal and colloquial uses of the terminology align more closely with how the terms are used (and not used) in Scripture. Words matter and create the pathways that we attempt to follow—for good or ill.

Second, the doctrine must be reconfigured around the balance and function of the biblical evidence for the different aspects of sanctification. In this book I have argued that the doctrine of sanctification should be reconfigured around the "accomplished" aspect or motif, because it sets the stage, provides the resources, determines the character, and thus controls the other motifs. Specifically, the imperatival and yet-to-be-completed aspects of sanctification must be seen in light of what God has already, decisively done to claim us,

1. I acknowledge that these are broad generalizations to which those I have in mind may object or want to insert nuances and qualifications. Nevertheless, I remain convinced that these generalizations accurately capture basic impulses and emphases, at least at a popular level. I have encountered and read too much of this pattern for too many years to be convinced otherwise.

cleanse us, and fit us for God's presence and purposes, all through Jesus Christ.

Third, the doctrinal profile must be vetted against how it actually affects Christians in the life of faith—the biblically enjoined pursuit of holiness. While experience is never a "stand-alone" criterion for truth, the multidimensional truthfulness of our doctrinal expressions is often exposed by patterns of experience as God's people try to live by what theologians and pastors tell them is true. Theological nearsightedness is matched or exceeded only by theological hubris if we who formulate and distribute doctrine refuse to pay attention to these patterns.

Accomplished sanctification has been overlooked in far too many Protestant evangelical circles, to the net effect that, tragically, doctrines of sanctification seem often to perplex, discourage, or bore as many Christians as they help. Theologians and biblical scholars cannot continue, as is sometimes our habit, to lay the blame on the people of God for not being as committed or as theologically interested as they should be. Although that can always be said of some, there is ample anecdotal evidence of serious, willing Christians whose spiritual journeys simply do not align with and are not assisted by the doctrinal paradigms given to them. Specifically, when the doctrine of sanctification is dominated by the sanctification imperatives, the somewhat oblique references to what is yet to be fulfilled, and the assumption that sanctification is synonymous with transformation, the stage is set for disheartening moralism that subtly replays spiritual toxicities of the medieval church against which the Reformers reacted.

Alternatively, when sanctification imperatives, promises, and the nature of spiritual transformation are positioned against the brilliant backlight of accomplished sanctification, then that which God has covenantally and personally accomplished in sanctification breathes life, power, and hope into the other aspects. We can and must be transformed; we can grow up in Christ, because we have been sanctified.

In a study such as this, there is the ever-present risk of trying to make the doctrine of sanctification do too much work. I acknowledge that risk and hope I have not done so. If I have, however, perhaps it will serve to highlight a treasure that has been overlooked. Close reexamination of what actually happens when God sanctifies us reminds us of what it means to be drawn into the dynamic presence of our Holy God, who, as the Holy One, is the Faithful One, and who makes provision for us to abide in the most intimate, life-giving proximity to God's own self. It refashions the questions we ask of God and of our own lives. It refocuses our attention and properly anchors our efforts. It resuscitates our hope in the God who has self-committed to us and graciously uses our lives for redemptive purposes.

# Bibliography


Alexander, Donald L., ed. *Christian Spirituality: Five Views of Sanctification*. Downers Grove, IL: InterVarsity, 1988.

Allen, Michael. *Sanctification*. New Studies in Dogmatics. Grand Rapids: Zondervan, 2017.

Allen, Ronald, and Gordon Borror. *Worship: Rediscovering the Missing Jewel*. Portland, OR: Multnomah, 1982.

Anderson, Ray S. *The Soul of Ministry: Forming Leaders for God's People*. Louisville: Westminster John Knox, 1997.

Arnold, Clinton E. *Ephesians*. Zondervan Exegetical Commentary on the New Testament. Grand Rapids: Zondervan, 2010.

Attridge, Harold W. *The Epistle to the Hebrews: A Commentary on the Epistle to the Hebrews*. Hermeneia. Philadelphia: Fortress, 1989.

Augustine. *On Christian Doctrine*. Translated by D. W. Robertson Jr. Indianapolis: Bobbs-Merrill, 1958.

Austin, J. L. *How to Do Things with Words*. New York: Oxford University Press, 1965.

Balthasar, Hans Urs von. *Engagement with God: The Drama of Christian Discipleship*. Translated by R. John Halliburton. 2nd ed. San Francisco: Ignatius, 2008.

Barabas, Steven. *So Great Salvation: The History and Message of the Keswick Convention*. London: Marshall, Morgan & Scott, 1952.

Barnett, Paul. *The Second Epistle to the Corinthians*. New International Commentary on the New Testament. Grand Rapids: Eerdmans, 1997.

Barth, Karl. *Church Dogmatics*. Vol. 3, part 4, *The Doctrine of Creation*. Edited by G. W. Bromiley and T. F. Torrance. 1961. Reprint, Peabody, MA: Hendrickson, 2010.

Bauckham, Richard J. "The Holiness of Jesus and His Disciples in the Gospel of John." In *Holiness and Ecclesiology in the New Testament*, edited by Kent E. Brower and Andy Johnson, 95–113. Grand Rapids: Eerdmans, 2007.

Belleville, Linda L. *2 Corinthians*. IVP New Testament Commentary. Downers Grove, IL: InterVarsity, 1996.

Bergen, Benjamin K. *Louder Than Words: The New Science of How the Mind Makes Meaning*. Philadelphia: Basic Books, 2012.

Berkouwer, G. C. *Faith and Sanctification*. Studies in Dogmatics. Grand Rapids: Eerdmans, 1952.

Billings, J. Todd. *Union with Christ: Reframing Theology and Ministry for the Church*. Grand Rapids: Baker Academic, 2011.

Bird, Michael F. *Evangelical Theology: A Biblical and Systematic Introduction*. Grand Rapids: Zondervan, 2013.

Bloesch, Donald G. *Theological Notebook*. 2 vols. Colorado Springs: Helmers & Howard, 1989–91.

Bonhoeffer, Dietrich. *Life Together*. Translated by John W. Doberstein. New York: Harper, 1954.

Bordwine, James E., ed. *A Guide to the Westminster Confession of Faith and Larger Catechism*. Jefferson, MD: Trinity Foundation, 1991.

Brown, Francis, S. R. Driver, and Charles A. Briggs. "קדשׁ." In *The Brown-Driver-Briggs Hebrew and English Lexicon*, 871–73. 1906. Reprint, Peabody, MA: Hendrickson, 2012.

Bruce, F. F. *The Epistle to the Hebrews*. New International Commentary on the New Testament. Grand Rapids: Eerdmans, 1964.

Bruckner, James K. *Exodus*. Understanding the Bible Commentary. Grand Rapids: Baker Books, 2012.

Buschart, W. David. *Exploring Protestant Traditions: An Invitation to Theological Hospitality*. Downers Grove, IL: IVP Academic, 2006.

Butler, Trent C. *Joshua*. Word Biblical Commentary. Waco: Word, 1983.

Calvin, John. *Institutes of the Christian Religion*. 2 vols. Edited by John T. McNeill. Translated by Ford Lewis Battles. Philadelphia: Westminster, 1960.

Carson, D. A. *The Gospel according to John*. Pillar New Testament Commentary. Grand Rapids: Eerdmans, 1991.

Chafer, Lewis Sperry. *He That Is Spiritual: A Classic Study of the Biblical Doctrine of Spirituality*. Rev. ed. Grand Rapids: Zondervan, 1967.

Childs, Brevard S. *The Book of Exodus: A Critical, Theological Commentary*. Old Testament Library. Louisville: Westminster, 1974.

Ciampa, Roy E., and Brian S. Rosner. *The First Letter to the Corinthians*. Pillar New Testament Commentary. Grand Rapids: Eerdmans, 2010.

Cockerill, Gareth Lee. *The Epistle to the Hebrews*. New International Commentary on the New Testament. Grand Rapids: Eerdmans, 2012.

Cohick, Lynn H. *Ephesians*. New Covenant Commentary. Eugene, OR: Cascade, 2010.

———. "We Are the Circumcision: Philippians 3 and the Christian Life." Lanier Theological Library, https://www.youtube.com/watch?v=Yz8n45yzEko.

Cranfield, C. E. B. *A Critical and Exegetical Commentary on the Epistle to the Romans*. 2 vols. International Critical Commentary. Edinburgh: T&T Clark, 1975.

Davids, Peter H. *The First Epistle of Peter*. New International Commentary on the New Testament. Grand Rapids: Eerdmans, 1990.

Davidson, Ivor J. "Gospel Holiness: Some Dogmatic Reflections." In *Sanctification: Explorations in Theology and Practice*, edited by Kelly M. Kapic, 189–211. Downers Grove, IL: IVP Academic, 2014.

Deddo, Gary W. *Karl Barth's Theology of Relations: Trinitarian, Christological, and Human; Towards an Ethic of the Family*. 2 vols. Eugene, OR: Wipf & Stock, 1999.

Demarest, Bruce. *Satisfy Your Soul: Restoring the Heart of Christian Spirituality*. Colorado Springs: NavPress, 1999.

———. *Seasons of the Soul: Stages of Spiritual Development*. Downers Grove, IL: IVP Books, 2009.

Dieter, Melvin E., Anthony A. Hoekema, Stanley M. Horton, J. Robertson McQuilkin, and John F. Walvoord. *Five Views on Sanctification*. Counterpoints. Grand Rapids: Zondervan, 1987.

Duhigg, Charles. *The Power of Habit: Why We Do What We Do in Life and Business*. New York: Random House, 2012.

Eilers, Kent, and Kyle C. Strobel, eds. *Sanctified by Grace: A Theology of the Christian Life*. London: Bloomsbury T&T Clark, 2014.

Elliott, John H. *1 Peter: A New Translation with Introduction and Commentary*. Anchor Bible. New York: Doubleday, 2000.

Fee, Gordon D. *The First Epistle to the Corinthians*. New International Commentary on the New Testament. Grand Rapids: Eerdmans, 1987.

Fitzmyer, Joseph A. *First Corinthians: A New Translation with Introduction and Commentary*. Anchor Yale Bible. New Haven: Yale University Press, 2008.

Forde, Gerhard O. "The Lutheran View." In *Christian Spirituality: Five Views of Sanctification*, edited by Donald L. Alexander, 13–46. Downers Grove, IL: InterVarsity, 1988.

Frame, John M. *Systematic Theology: An Introduction to Christian Belief*. Phillipsburg, NJ: P&R, 2013.

Furnish, Victor Paul. *Theology and Ethics in Paul*. Introduction by Richard B. Hays. New Testament Library. Louisville: Westminster John Knox, 2009.

Garland, David E. *1 Corinthians*. Baker Exegetical Commentary on the New Testament. Grand Rapids: Baker Academic, 2003.

———. *2 Corinthians*. New American Commentary. Nashville: Broadman & Holman, 1999.

Gentry, Peter J. "The Meaning of 'Holy' in the Old Testament." *Bibliotheca Sacra* 170 (October–December 2013): 400–417.

Grane, Leif. *The Augsburg Confession: A Commentary*. Translated by John H. Rasmussen. Minneapolis: Augsburg, 1987.

Greathouse, William M. *From the Apostles to Wesley: Christian Perfection in Historical Perspective*. Kansas City, MO: Beacon Hill, 1979.

Grenz, Stanley J. *The Named God and the Question of Being: A Trinitarian Theo-Ontology*. Louisville: Westminster John Knox, 2005.

———. *The Social God and the Relational Self: A Trinitarian Theology of the* Imago Dei. Louisville: Westminster John Knox, 2001.

Grudem, Wayne. *Systematic Theology: An Introduction to Biblical Doctrine*. Grand Rapids: Zondervan, 1994.

Gupta, Nijay K. *1–2 Thessalonians*. New Covenant Commentary. Eugene, OR: Cascade, 2016.

Guthrie, George H. *2 Corinthians*. Baker Exegetical Commentary on the New Testament. Grand Rapids: Baker Academic, 2015.

Harrington, Bobby, and Josh Patrick. *The Disciple Maker's Handbook: Seven Elements of a Discipleship Lifestyle*. Grand Rapids: Zondervan, 2017.

Harris, Murray J. *Colossians and Philemon*. Exegetical Guide to the Greek New Testament: Nashville: B&H Academic, 2010.

———. *The Second Epistle to the Corinthians: A Commentary on the Greek Text*. New International Greek Text Commentary. Grand Rapids: Eerdmans, 2005.

Howard, Evan B. *A Guide to Christian Spiritual Formation: How Scripture, Spirit, Community, and Mission Shape Our Souls*. Grand Rapids: Baker Academic, 2018.

Howard, James M. *Paul, the Community, and Progressive Sanctification: An Exploration into Community-Based Transformation within Pauline Theology*. Studies in Biblical Literature. New York: Peter Lang, 2007.

Hull, Bill. *The Complete Book of Discipleship: On Being and Making Followers of Jesus Christ*. Colorado Springs: NavPress, 2006.

Jobes, Karen H. *1 Peter*. Baker Exegetical Commentary on the New Testament. Grand Rapids: Baker Academic, 2005.

Kapic, Kelly M., ed. *Sanctification: Explorations in Theology and Practice*. Downers Grove, IL: IVP Academic, 2014.

Keener, Craig S. *The Gospel of John: A Commentary*. 2 vols. Peabody, MA: Hendrickson, 2003.

———. *The Mind of the Spirit: Paul's Approach to Transformed Thinking*. Grand Rapids: Baker Academic, 2016.

Kelsey, David H. *Eccentric Existence: A Theological Anthropology*. 2 vols. Louisville: Westminster John Knox, 2009.

Kilner, John F. *Dignity and Destiny: Humanity in the Image of God*. Grand Rapids: Eerdmans, 2015.

Lane, Belden C. *The Solace of Fierce Landscapes: Exploring Desert and Mountain Spirituality*. Oxford: Oxford University Press, 1998.

Leithart, Peter J. *1 & 2 Kings*. Brazos Theological Commentary on the Bible. Grand Rapids: Brazos, 2006.

Levering, Matthew. *Engaging the Doctrine of the Holy Spirit: Love and Gift in the Trinity and the Church*. Grand Rapids: Baker Academic, 2016.

Lewis, Gordon R., and Bruce A. Demarest. *Integrative Theology*. 3 vols. Grand Rapids: Zondervan, 1996.

Lincoln, Andrew T. *Ephesians*. Word Biblical Commentary. Nashville: Thomas Nelson, 1990.

Lints, Richard. "Living by Faith—Alone? Reformed Responses to Antinomianism." In *Sanctification: Explorations in Theology and Practice*, edited by Kelly M. Kapic, 35–56. Downers Grove, IL: IVP Academic, 2014.

Longenecker, Richard N. *The Epistle to the Romans: A Commentary on the Greek Text*. New International Greek Text Commentary. Grand Rapids: Eerdmans, 2016.

Luther, Martin. *Commentaries on 1 Corinthians 7, 1 Corinthians 15, Lectures on 1 Timothy*. Vol. 28 of *Luther's Works*. Edited by Hilton C. Oswald. St. Louis: Concordia, 1973.

———. *Commentary on the Epistle to the Romans*. Translated by J. Theodore Mueller. Grand Rapids: Zondervan, 1954.

———. *Lectures on Romans*. Vol. 25 of *Luther's Works*. Edited by Hilton C. Oswald. St. Louis: Concordia, 1972.

———. *A Short Explanation of Dr. Martin Luther's Small Catechism: A Handbook of Christian Doctrine*. Rev. ed. St. Louis: Concordia, 1965.

Mackinnon, James. *Luther and the Reformation*. Vol. 1, *Early Life and Religious Development to 1517*. New York: Russell & Russell, 1962.

Maddox, Randy L. *Responsible Grace: John Wesley's Practical Theology*. Nashville: Abingdon, 1994.

Malherbe, Abraham J. *The Letters to the Thessalonians: A New Translation with Introduction and Commentary*. Anchor Bible. New York: Doubleday, 2000.

Mannermaa, Tuomo. *Christ Present in Faith: Luther's View of Justification*. Minneapolis: Fortress, 2005.

Marsden, George M. *Fundamentalism and American Culture: The Shaping of Twentieth-Century Evangelicalism, 1870–1925*. New York: Oxford University Press, 1980.

Martin, Ralph P. *The Worship of God: Some Theological, Pastoral, and Practical Reflections*. Grand Rapids: Eerdmans, 1982.

Mbuvi, Andrew M. *Jude and 2 Peter*. New Covenant Commentary. Eugene, OR: Cascade, 2015.

McGrath, Alister. *To Know and Serve God: A Biography of James I. Packer*. London: Hodder & Stoughton, 1997.

McKnight, Scot. *The Letter to the Colossians*. New International Commentary on the New Testament. Grand Rapids: Eerdmans, 2017.

Meek, Esther Lightcap. *Loving to Know: Covenantal Epistemology*. Eugene, OR: Cascade, 2011.

Meyers, Carol. *Exodus*. New Cambridge Bible Commentary. New York: Cambridge University Press, 2005.

Mitchell, Basil. *How to Play Theological Ping-Pong: And Other Essays on Faith and Reason*. Grand Rapids: Eerdmans, 1990.

Moo, Douglas. *The Epistle to the Romans*. New International Commentary on the New Testament. Grand Rapids: Eerdmans, 1996.

Mulholland, M. Robert, Jr. *The Deeper Journey: The Spirituality of Discovering Your True Self*. Downers Grove, IL: IVP Books, 2006.

———. *Shaped by the Word: The Power of Scripture in Spiritual Formation*. Rev. ed. Nashville: Upper Room, 2000.

Murray, John. "Definitive Sanctification." *Calvin Theological Journal* 2, no. 1 (April 1967): 5–21.

Nelson, Richard D. *Joshua*. Old Testament Library. Louisville: Westminster John Knox, 1997.

Ngewa, Samuel M. *1 & 2 Timothy and Titus*. Africa Bible Commentary. Grand Rapids: Zondervan, 2009.

Noble, T. A. *Holy Trinity: Holy People; The Theology of Christian Perfecting*. Cambridge: James Clarke, 2013.

Oswalt, John N. *Called to Be Holy: A Biblical Perspective*. Anderson, IN: Francis Asbury, 1999.

Outler, Albert C. "The Wesleyan Quadrilateral—In John Wesley." *Wesleyan Theological Journal* 20, no. 1 (Spring 1985): 7–18.

Owen, John. *The Works of John Owen*. 23 vols. Edited by William H. Goold. 1850–53. Reprint, Edinburgh: The Banner of Truth Trust, 1967.

Packer, J. I. "Evangelical Foundations of Spirituality." In *The Collected Shorter Writings of J. I. Packer*. Vol. 2, *Serving the People of God*, 255–67. Carlisle, UK: Paternoster, 1998.

———. "'Keswick' and the Reformed Doctrine of Sanctification." *Evangelical Quarterly* 27 (1955): 153–67.

Patterson, Kerry, Joseph Grenny, David Maxfield, Ron McMillan, and Al Switzler. *Change Anything: The New Science of Personal Success*. New York: Business Plus, 2011.

Payne, Don J. *The Theology of the Christian Life in J. I. Packer's Thought: Theological Anthropology, Theological Method, and the Doctrine of Sanctification*. Studies in Evangelical History and Thought. Milton Keynes, UK: Paternoster, 2006.

Perkins, Pheme. *First Corinthians*. Paideia Commentaries on the New Testament. Grand Rapids: Baker Academic, 2012.

Peterson, David. *Possessed by God: A New Testament Theology of Sanctification and Holiness*. New Studies in Biblical Theology. Grand Rapids: Eerdmans, 1995.

Piper, John. *The Future of Justification: A Response to N. T. Wright*. Wheaton: Crossway, 2007.

Placher, William C. *A History of Christian Theology: An Introduction*. Philadelphia: Westminster, 1983.

Powlison, David. *How Does Sanctification Work?* Wheaton: Crossway, 2017.

Reid, Stephen Breck. "Psalm 50: Prophetic Speech." In *Prophets and Paradigms: Essays in Honor of Gene M. Tucker*, edited by Stephen Breck Reid, 217–30. Journal for the Study of the Old Testament Supplement Series. Sheffield: Sheffield Academic Press, 1996.

Robertson, O. Palmer. *The Books of Nahum, Habakkuk, and Zephaniah*. New International Commentary on the Old Testament. Grand Rapids: Eerdmans, 1990.

Rutledge, Fleming. *The Crucifixion: Understanding the Death of Jesus Christ*. Grand Rapids: Eerdmans, 2015.

Schreiner, Thomas R. *1, 2 Peter, Jude*. New American Commentary. Nashville: Broadman & Holman, 2003.

Schroeder, H. J., ed. *Canons and Decrees of the Council of Trent*. St. Louis: B. Herder, 1941.

Searle, John R. *Speech Acts: An Essay in the Philosophy of Language*. Cambridge: Cambridge University Press, 1970.

Sifers, Steven C. "The Armor of God: Ephesians 6:10–20." MA thesis, Denver Seminary, 2018.

Smith, Gordon T. *Called to Be Saints: An Invitation to Christian Maturity*. Downers Grove, IL: IVP Academic, 2014.

Smith, Hannah Whitall. *The Christian's Secret to a Happy Life*. Chicago: Revell, 1883.

Smith, James K. A. *You Are What You Love: The Spiritual Power of Habit*. Grand Rapids: Brazos, 2016.

Strobel, Kyle. "Sanctified in the Son: The Contours of the Doctrine of Sanctification." Paper presented at the 66th Annual Meeting of the Evangelical Theological Society, San Diego, CA, November 19–21, 2014.

Stuart, Douglas K. *Exodus*. New American Commentary. Nashville: B&H, 2006.

Tappert, Theodore G., trans. and ed. *The Book of Concord: The Confessions of the Evangelical Lutheran Church*. Philadelphia: Fortress, 1959.

Thielicke, Helmut. *The Evangelical Faith*. Vol. 1, *Prolegomena: The Relation of Theology to Modern Thought-Forms*. Translated and edited by Geoffrey W. Bromiley. Grand Rapids: Eerdmans, 1974.

Thiselton, Anthony C. *The First Epistle to the Corinthians: A Commentary on the Greek Text*. New International Greek Testament Commentary. Grand Rapids: Eerdmans, 2000.

———. *New Horizons in Hermeneutics: The Theory and Practice of Transforming Biblical Reading*. Grand Rapids: Zondervan, 1992.

Thomas Aquinas. *Summa Theologica*. 2nd ed. Translated by Fathers of the English Dominican Province. London: Burns Oates & Washbourne, 1927.

Thrall, Bill, Bruce McNicol, and John Lynch. *Truefaced: Trust God and Others with Who You Really Are*. Colorado Springs: NavPress, 2003.

Toon, Peter. *Justification and Sanctification*. Foundations for Faith. Westchester, IL: Crossway, 1983.

Torrance, T. F. *Atonement*. Edited by Robert T. Walker. Downers Grove, IL: IVP Academic, 2009.

———. *The Trinitarian Faith*. 2nd ed. London: T&T Clark, 1997.

Tournier, Paul. *The Adventure of Living*. Translated by Edwin Hudson. New York: Harper & Row, 1965.

Towner, Philip H. *The Letters to Timothy and Titus*. New International Commentary on the New Testament. Grand Rapids: Eerdmans, 2006.

Van De Walle, Bernie A. *Rethinking Holiness: A Theological Introduction*. Grand Rapids: Baker Academic, 2017.

Vang, Preben. *1 Corinthians*. Teach the Text Commentary. Grand Rapids: Baker Books, 2014.

Vanhoozer, Kevin J. *The Drama of Doctrine: A Canonical-Linguistic Approach to Christian Revelation*. Louisville: Westminster John Knox, 2005.

Wanamaker, Charles A. *The Epistles to the Thessalonians: A Commentary on the Greek Text*. New International Greek Text Commentary. Grand Rapids: Eerdmans, 1990.

Webster, John. *Holiness*. Grand Rapids: Eerdmans, 2003.

Weima, Jeffrey A. D. *1–2 Thessalonians*. Baker Exegetical Commentary on the New Testament. Grand Rapids: Baker Academic, 2014.

Wesley, John. *A Plain Account of Christian Perfection*. London: Epworth, 1952.

Willard, Dallas. *The Great Omission: Reclaiming Jesus's Essential Teachings on Discipleship*. New York: HarperOne, 2006.

———. *Renovation of the Heart: Putting on the Character of Christ*. Colorado Springs: NavPress, 2002.

Wright, N. T. *Justification: God's Plan and Paul's Vision*. Downers Grove, IL: IVP Academic, 2009.

Young, Mark. "Recapturing Evangelical Identity and Mission." In *Still Evangelical? Insiders Reconsider Political, Social, and Theological Meaning*, edited by Mark Labberton, 46–65. Downers Grove, IL: InterVarsity, 2018.

# Scripture Index

# Subject Index

Printed and bound by CPI Group (UK) Ltd, Croydon, CR0 4YY

13/04/2025

14656457-0002